ORIGINAL SIN

in the Light of

MODERN SCIENCE

Rev. Patrick O'Connell, B.D.

LUMEN CHRISTI PRESS
P.O. Box 13176
Houston, Texas 77019

Third printing: September 1973

NIHIL OBSTAT:
✠Robert J. Dwyer, D.D., Ph.D.
Archbishop of Portland, Oregon

IMPRIMATUR:
✠Robert J. Dwyer, D.D., Ph.D.
Archbishop of Portland, Oregon

ISBN 0-912414-15-4

Printed in the United States of America

Table Of Contents

PART I

Table Of Contents

PART II

Publisher's Note

When Father Patrick O'Connell died in the Spring of 1971 he was 87 years of age. Right up to a day or two before his death he was continuing his work to make the truth known. Actually, he was already dead when I received the last letter he wrote to me, in which he again urged me to try to distribute widely this little book, knowing full well that I considered it a must for anyone who takes life and death seriously. Even then, more than two years ago, I wanted to present the book in a more attractive form than the original publication. A second printing, made available after the author's death, is now out of print. Eventually I secured the rights to make sure that copies will always be available. The reader will find that the material contained in so few pages is invaluable.

During Vatican II, the author presented a copy of the Italian translation of his larger work, *Science of Today and the Problem of Genesis* (a book defending the inerrancy of the Bible) to His Holiness, Pope Paul VI. During the Synod of Bishops in 1969, he presented to the Holy Father the Italian translation of this book (defending the teaching of the Church against the Neo-Modernists). In recognition of these services to the Church

His Holiness conferred on Father O'Connell the honor *Pro Ecclesia Et Pontifice.*

Father O'Connell writes in a clear and easy to read style, recounting and considering carefully the scientific discoveries of recent years. From a comparative examination the author draws the conclusion that the great scientists of the past century have furnished proofs in support of the biblical account of the origin of man and of the manner of life of earliest man; that they have also furnished proof in support of the traditional teaching of the Church that the human race is descended from a single pair of ancestors.

He shows that the theory which alleges that man was evolved from a lower animal is now no longer tenable and that the theory of polygenism which the Modernists link with the theory of evolution collapses with it.

We hope that the book will be widely read so that the author's, as well as the Holy Father's, wishes will be fulfilled. Then my promise to the author will be fulfilled also.

W. Doyle Gilligan

Preface

This small book is intended to serve as a supplement to my book entitled "The Origin and Early History of Man" which is now being printed. For the convenience of the reader the scientific information about the Ice Age, the Great Flood which brought the Ice Age to a close, the fossil remains of man and the amended theory of evolution called Neo-Darwinism is repeated in this book.

The purpose of this book is to show that the evidence, produced in the name of science for the theory of plurality of ancestors of the human race called polygenism by those Catholic writers who hold the theory, has all been proved to consist of mere unproven hypotheses devoid of real scientific foundation and that the real scientific evidence which has come to light during the present century supports the traditional teaching of the Catholic Church on the origin of man, the unity of the human race and the doctrine of Original Sin.

The scientific information contained in this book is taken from my larger work *Science of Today and the Problems of Genesis* (364 pp.) for the composition of which all the principal books on the subject discussed, in English, French, Italian, Spanish and German have been consulted. An abbreviated edition of this work has been translated into Italian, French and Spanish. The Italian edition was presented to His Holiness Pope Paul VI, and was reviewed in *L'Osservatore Romano* on

July 11, 1964. The following is an extract from this review:

The thesis of this book is that Palaeontology furnishes us with an irrefutable argument in favour of the traditional teaching of the Church, that no genetic link between man and beast exists, but that the body of man was formed by God in a special manner. The book is, therefore, in complete agreement with the teaching of the Encyclical (of Pope Pius XII) *Humani generis*.

The book is the result of fifty years reading and study. The author shows that the biological arguments for evolution used in books by present-day evolutionists, even in Italy, have been discarded by leading scientists, and even by atheists such as the late Julian Huxley, and that their most important argument, which is based on fossils alleged by them to be half-man and half-beast, has collapsed completely. In particular, the author shows that the famous "missing links"—the Neanderthal Man, the Java Man, the Peking Man, (which Fr. Teilhard de Chardin uses as one of his principal arguments for his fantastic theories), the Australopithecine fossils and even the Oreopithecus of Baccinello—were in fact all cases of deception and fraud. The remaining "missing links" were either counterfeited artificially or belong to apes and monkeys and not to men. . . .

PATRICK O'CONNELL.

PART 1

The Teaching of the Catholic Church on the Origin of Man, the Unity of the Human Race and Original Sin Vindicated by The Scientific Discoveries of the Present Century

The Scientific Discoveries

Remarkable and, indeed, sensational discoveries have been made during the past century by geologists, palaeontologists and archaeologists which provide an immense amount of accurate information on the questions of the origin and early history of man, but a combination of circumstances has prevented these discoveries from reaching the general public or even professors in universities and major seminaries.

Geology and palaeontology are regarded as subjects too difficult for ordinary learned men. Hence, most authors of books on the problems of the first eleven chapters of Genesis, which deal with such fundamental doctrines as the unity of the human race and Original Sin, think themselves justified

1

in getting their information at second-hand from popular books, most of which are written by atheists, and excuse themselves from making independent investigation by consulting the books written by the recognized experts on these subjects.

Then there is the fact that, as the result of a century of propaganda, evolutionists have acquired influence over the press and the book-trade, and being aware that these recent discoveries provide strong arguments against their evolutionistic theories, do all in their power to keep these discoveries from being known. Finally, there is the fact that we have had two World Wars during the present century which have distracted attention from the discoveries, and interrupted scientific investigations.

The Discoveries Concerning The Early History Of Man, Made Before The First World War

The two most important of these discoveries were, the discovery of the cause, extent and date of the Glacial Period, and of the fact that a great flood occurred on the last year of this Glacial Period.

These two events—the zero year of the Glacial Periods (or Period) and the great flood which occurred the same year—are intimately connected, as we shall see, and provide the best clue that we have, to the early history of man.

The cause of the Glacial Period or Ice Age, which had been a subject of much controversy, is now known to have been the elevation of the Northern Hemisphere above the snow line, with the result that the snow which fell did not melt but continued accumulating until it reached a height of from one to two miles. The end of the Ice Age was caused by the gradual sinking down of the Northern Hemisphere under the burden of ice, during a period which lasted thousands of years until it sank beneath the ocean, with the result that warm water of the ocean rushed in and finished off the melting of the ice in a few months, after which, the part depressed rose slowly again. This is a phenomenon which occurred periodically in the course of geological history; depressions of small areas have occurred many times as the result of earthquakes since this last major depression, but never on the same vast scale as the depression at the end of the Ice Age period.

The discovery of the date of the zero year of the last Glacial Period was made by Baron de Geer of Sweden and Mateo Sauramo of Finland, by the method known as the varve-analysis method. As the sudden ending of the protracted melting of the ice was caused by the inrush of the water from the ocean, the date of the Great Flood naturally coincided with the zero year of the Ice Age. The date of these two events was calculated to be approximately 7,000 B.C. This calculation has been confirmed by Carbon 14 tests, carried out on materials found both immediately above and below the deposits left by the Great Flood over the ancient cities of the Middle East.

The most remarkable confirmation of the date, 7,000 B.C., was found at Jericho during the excavation of the pre-flood city, about ten years ago, where charred wood (the most suitable material for Carbon 14 tests) found both above and below the flood deposit was tested, and the age was ascertained to be approximately 7,000 B.C.

The salt water in the Dead Sea, which is only about two miles from Jericho, was, according to geologists, left behind by the same Great Flood because there was no outlet to the ocean. The Carbon 14 tests carried out at Jericho, therefore, besides fixing the date of the destruction of Jericho fix also the date at which the salt water was deposited in the Dead Sea, as being also 7,000 B.C.

Discoveries By Archaeologists

While the geologists were at work at the end of the last century, the archaeologists began the excavation of the ancient pre-flood cities, first in Egypt and soon afterwards in Turkestan, in Asia, 300 miles east of the Caspian Sea.

In Egypt, the post-flood treasures found in the tombs of the Pharoes attracted most attention; however, artifacts of great perfection such as beautifully painted pottery and copper instruments were found in the pre-flood stratum. Great numbers of pre-flood human skeletons were found in the arid desert along the upper Nile, but these attracted little attention because they resembled the skeletons of modern man.

In Turkestan, the ancient cities which were excavated resembled the ancient cities of Mesopotamia in that these cities showed the flood deposit separating the pre-flood and post-flood strata. An account of these excavations will be found in *Excavations in Turkestan* (2 vols. 1904) by Raphael Pumpelly.

According to Pumpelly's calculations, the great flood occurred about 6,000 B.C. (which is not far from the date arrived at by Baron de Geer). He calculated also, that from the earliest settlement in Turkestan to the time of the flood about 3,000 years elapsed during which the progress in the making of utensils and tools could be traced from the first primitive instruments to the beautiful painted pottery and hammered copper weapons found in the stratum just beneath the flood deposits. There were found also the fossil remains of the common domestic animals, the ox, the pig, the horse, and the sheep, as well as some barley and wheat. These facts provide conclusive evidence that tool-making, agriculture and stock-raising were practiced by earliest man. Thus the geologists and archaeologists at the beginning of the present century found a practical solution for the problem of the origin and early history of man, which is in perfect accord with the accounts given in the first chapters of Genesis.

The war between Turkey and the Balkan States and the First World War, which followed it, interrupted the excavations and distracted attention from the results achieved by the geologists and archaeologists.

Readers who wish to get more detailed information about the scientific discoveries concerning the origin and early history of man are referred to my larger work, *Science of Today and the Problems of Genesis.*

The Discoveries Made Since The First World War Up To The Present Time

The books written by geologists since the First World War have added little to our knowledge of the origin and early history of man; books by English and American geologists, like the books by Sir Henry Howorth, which were regarded as being unfavorable to the theory of evolution, were allowed to go into oblivion without ever reaching the Continent of Europe, while the books by German authors Penck and Bruckner, which favored the theory of evolution, made their way into the universities of Rome, and from Rome the theory of Penck and Bruckner about the four Glacial Periods with three warm intervals (during which man was alleged to have existed) was carried back to Ireland, England and America by students who had studied at Rome. However, at present, after a dark period of forty years, the discoveries made by scientists before the First World War are beginning to be known.

By the time the archaeologists resumed the work of excavating of the ancient cities of the Middle East many of the great scientists had died and their books were forgotten.

The object of the new expeditions was more to find the treasures buried in the ancient cities of the Babylonian and Assyrian Empires, than to obtain information about the early history of man; but whatever may have been the motives of the men who took part in them, besides providing the museums of various countries with works of art of unexpected elegance, they put at the disposal of scholars sufficient information to enable them to trace the history of mankind back to the earliest man.

The following is a summary of the principal results obtained by the men who carried out the excavations:

(1) The information given in the books published by the geologists and archaeologists before the First World War, about the fact that a great flood had occurred about 7,000 B.C. and that it covered a great part of the Northern Hemisphere was confirmed by men who had never seen or heard of the books by pre-war authors, such as Sir Henry Howorth, F.R.S., or of Raphael Pumpelly.

(2) The information derived from the excavations that have been carried out since the First World War to the present day is sufficient to enable anyone who takes the trouble of collecting and collating it to draw a map showing the towns and cities built before the Great Flood and even the caves in which the nomadic tribes, such as the Neanderthal tribe, sheltered.

It is now known that the Neanderthal man who had practically a monopoly of the hunting in Europe and in Africa south of Egypt, which was uninhabited before the Great Flood, was contemporaneous with dwellers in the towns and cities of the Middle East who manufactured beautiful pottery, copper utensils and weapons, and who tilled the land and kept domestic animals.

The Excavations Carried Out During The Past Century On The Sites Of The Pre-Flood Cities Of The Middle East

These excavations were carried out by organized expeditions from various countries, and have been going on for nearly a century. Accounts of them were published at the time that these excavations were carried out, but the books containing these accounts are either out of print or difficult to obtain. A few books, such as *The Bible as History*, which purport to give a summary of the results of the excavations have been published, but these books confine themselves to accounts of the post-Flood period with only one chapter on the pre-Flood period, which almost invariably contains the misleading information that the most important results were obtained at Ur of the Chaldees and Kish, near ancient Babylon; that the excavations at these places showed that the flood was confined to Mesopotamia; and that the date was 4,000 B.C. These misleading accounts of excavations carried out now nearly forty years ago are still found in some present-day books by Catholic authors.

The men chiefly responsible for these misleading accounts are Sir Leonard Woolley, who superintended the excavations at Ur of the Chaldees and who wrote his account in *Ur of the Chaldees* and afterwards in *Excavations at Ur*, and Andre Parrot, the author of *Noah's Ark*. Both of these men gave as their opinion that the flood was confined to Mesopotamia and that the date was about 4,000 B.C.

In his two books, Sir Leonard Woolley gives most valuable information about the life of man both before and after the flood, and he makes it clear that his statements about the extent and date of the floor are only conjectures: the book, *Noah's Ark*, by Parrot, contains no new scientific information, but several errors, and appears to have been written with the express object of contradicting the Mosaic account and defending the account given by those who adopt the Wellhausen theory of the four different sources of Genesis.

However, during the forty years that have elapsed since Sir Leonard Woolley began the excavations at Ur, the work of excavating the towns and cities of the Middle East has continued with just one interruption during the Second World War, and it can now be confidently asserted that we now know the various places that were inhabited by man before the Flood; that we know all the principal towns and cities that were built and even the location of the caves in Europe and Africa where the nomadic races such as the Neanderthal, who lived by hunting, sheltered.

The Excavations At Jericho, Tepe Gawra And On The High Plateau Of Iran

Both Ur of the Chaldees and Kish, near ancient Babylon, are situated on ground not much above sea level, and hence no indication can be obtained from excavations carried out at them of the extent of the Flood; they were built at a comparatively recent period before the Flood, and could not provide information about the manner of life of earliest man. The really important pre-Flood cities are Jericho, Tepe Gawra not far from Nineveh, and the cities of the high Plateau of Iran, firstly, because they could not be reached by a local flood in Mesopotamia, and secondly, because their foundation goes back to the time of earliest man and, therefore, they can give a good idea of the manner of his life.

The following is a brief account of the results obtained from the excavations at each of these three places: [1]

(1) In my larger work *Science of Today and the Problems of Genesis,* I have dealt in considerable detail with the excavations carried out during the present century in the parts of the world inhabited by the human race before the Great Flood at the end of the Ice Age.
See note on Noe's Ark, page 108.

The Excavations Carried Out At Jericho

Jericho is situated less than two miles from the Dead Sea, the salt water of which was brought from the ocean by the Great Flood which occurred in 7,000 B.C. and left behind because the Dead Sea is far below the level of the ocean. Jericho is one of the first cities built by man: it had its origin probably about 3,000 years before the Flood. It was rebuilt after it and continued for another 5,500 years until it was burned by Josue. Excavations were begun by a German expedition before the First World War, but had to be suspended. They were resumed in 1929 by a British expedition under Professor Garstang and continued until 1936. They were resumed again after the Second World War by an expedition under Dr. Kathleen Kenyon and continued until a few years ago. It was only during the last two expeditions that traces of the Great Flood were discovered.

Both Professor Garstang and Dr. Kathleen Kenyon have written books giving the results of the excavations. While their accounts differ about the date of the destruction of the city of Josue, because they followed different systems of chronology, they are in complete agreement in the descriptions of the pre-Flood city, its destruction by water, its being abandoned for a long period after the flood and of the standard of civilization reached at the time of the flood. Both accounts are in agreement in saying that the pre-flood inhabitants had manufactured household utensils and agricultural instruments of a distinctive type, different from those found in the pre-flood cities of Mesopotamia that they appeared to have lived in splendid isolation until a short time before the flood when the wares of Egypt and Mesopotamia, which were of superior quality, began to be imported. Because of the fact that evidence of the cultivation of the land and the keeping of domestic animals—which did not commence in Europe until the Neolithic Age (4,000-3,000 B.C.)—was found in the course of excavations, both Garstang and Kathleen Kenyon came to the erroneous conclusion that the pre-flood city of Jericho must have belonged to the Neolithic Age, in spite of the fact that all the stone instruments found were made according to the Paleolithic method which is by flaking. When, however, tests by the Carbon 14 method were applied to charred wood, which was found in abundance both below and above the flood deposit, it was discovered that the date of the destruction of the pre-flood city was about 7,000 B.C., the date given by geologists at which the salt was carried to the Dead Sea from the ocean by the Great Flood at the end of the Ice Age.

The Excavations At Tepe Gawra

Tepe Gawra is situated on the high ground to the northeast of the ancient city of Nineveh. As it is about 2,000 feet above sea level it could not have been reached by a mere local flood. Excavations that were carried out just before the Second World War have revealed that there had been an ancient city built long before the flood; that it was destroyed by the flood, abandoned for an indefinite period and then rebuilt; that there had been in all 26 occupational levels, which indicated that the city had been built, abandoned and rebuilt 26 times; that ten of these occupational levels were beneath the flood deposits and 16 above it; that the pottery and artifacts found in the pre-flood strata were much superior to those found at Jericho. The kilns in which the beautifully painted pre-flood pottery was baked were found in the stratum just immediately below the flood deposit. In the same stratum utensils and weapons made by hammering open cast copper were also found. In the strata immediately above the flood deposit, there was no pottery or copper instruments but only rough flint implements. Man, after the Flood, had to begin again.

The Plateau At Iran

The Plateau of Iran is more than 5,000 feet above the plain of Mesopotamia. Part of the Plateau consists of a salt desert, the salt of which was brought in from the ocean 7,000 B.C. by the same flood that deposited the salt in the Dead Sea. Excavations carried out on the Plateau after the Second World War have revealed that there had been a number of flourishing towns on the remaining part of the Plateau; that these had been destroyed by a flood; that the standard of material civilization reached before the flood was the highest in the Middle East; that copper utensils and weapons had been manufactured in considerable quantity before the flood by hammering the copper with the natural alloy that it contained; and that the copper had been mined on the slopes of the mountains of Iran.[1]

Evidence Of The Extent Of The Flood From The Frozen Carcasses Of Mammoths Found Along The Shores Of The Arctic Ocean

As there is no mountain range or other obstacle between the Plateau of Iran and the Arctic Ocean, a flood that covered the Plateau and the sides of the adjacent mountains would have reached not only the Arctic Ocean but also Canada and the North of America, and there is convincing evidence that it actually reached these places. In his book, *The Mammoth and the Flood* published in 1887,

(1) The Bible tells us that Cain went to the East after the murder of Abel, and that Tubalcain, his descendant, was a hammerer of brass and iron (i.e. of metal). The excavations on the Plateau of Iran provide an indication that Cain (and his wife or wives, who were his sisters) may have gone to Iran. There is a tradition which is supported by private revelations that Adam and Eve went to Palestine after the Fall, and that Seth was born there and that Adam was buried at Calvary. The Bible represents the descendants of Cain as making greater progress in the manufacturing arts than the descendants of Seth; the articrafts found in the pre-Flood cities of Iran are definitely superior to those found in the pre-Flood strata of Jericho. The excavations do not prove these facts but they support them.

Sir Henry Howorth tells us that whole herds of mammoths of all ages, from full-grown specimens to baby mammoths, were found along the coast line of the Arctic Ocean in the islands near the coast and in various other places in Siberia, and that some of these had even the skin and hair intact and were so perfectly preserved that their flesh can still be eaten. The warm water carried from the ocean by the flood at the same time drowned whole herds of these huge beasts and melted the ice along the Arctic Ocean, and when it returned to the ocean the water soon froze over the mammoths and has never thawed again up to the present day. Both Sir Henry Howorth and G. F. Wright gave evidence to show that the Great Flood covered not only Canada, but the United States as far south as the valley of the Mississippi.

Scientific Discoveries In Connection With The Theory Of Evolution.

Attempted Discoveries

Jean Baptist Lamarck of France (1744-1829) and Charles Darwin of England (1809-1882) were among the first who endeavored to explain the origin of the various species of living things, including the origin of man, by the theory of evolution. Lamarck taught that God created a number of primitive living organisms and that from them the various species of living things now existing were gradually evolved through the influence of environment, and that the improvement thus acquired was transmitted to the descendants of these living things.

Charles Darwin in *The Origin of Species*, the book in which he explained his theory, taught that evolution was accomplished through the operation of three mysterious forces: Natural Selection, Struggle for Existence, and Survival of the Fittest. With regard to the origin of man, Darwin taught in his *Descent of Man* that man, who is the last of the series was evolved directly from an ape. At the time of the publicatoin of *The Origin of Species*, Darwin professed belief in God, but after the publication of *The Descent of Man* when he had secured the support of prominent atheists who saw that his theory could be used to propagate atheism, he announced that he had ceased to believe in God. In his original theory Darwin taught that the Creator breathed mysterious powers into a few forms or into one; but in its final form, he taught that all living things could be traced back to one form which arose by spontaneous generation.

In the tenth chapter of *The Origin of Species*, Darwin admitted that the only direct proof of his theory would be the existence of the fossils of a series of intermediate forms or links showing the gradual evolution of species ending with man, and that if such a series of fossils could not be found, his theory would collapse. He admitted also that such a series of fossils had not been found, that the sudden appearance of all the species of invertebrates in the Cambrian rocks and the subsequent sudden appearance of the various species of vertebrates at long intervals, could not be explained by his theory at the time that he wrote, but gave the excuse that the geological record was imperfect, and expressed the hope that the required series of fossils would be found.

His followers have been compelled to make the admission—that a series of fossils of intermediate forms constitute the only direct proof of Darwin's theory—and seeing that it is imperative to find them, they have made claims periodically during the centuries since Darwin's time to have found them but, as we shall see, these claims have been refuted. The original theories of both Lamarck and Darwin have long since been abandoned and have been replaced by Neo-Lamarckism, which is very little known and Neo-Darwinism, the present prevailing theory of evolutionists.

The late Sir Julian Huxley, on page 40 of his book, *Evolution in Action* (published in 1953), has the following commentary on these abandoned systems which had been accepted by so-called progressive Catholic authors for more than half a century.

"With the knowledge which has been amassed since Darwin's time, it is no longer possible to believe that evolution is brought about through the so-called inheritance of acquired characteristics— the direct effects of the use and misuse of organs, or of the changes of environment; or by the conscious of unconscious will of organisms; or through the mysterious operations of some vital force; or by any other inherent tendency.

"All the theories lumped together under the heads of orthogenesis and Lamarckism are invalidated. . . . in the light of modern discoveries, they no longer deserve to be called scientific theories, but can be called speculations without due basis of reality, or superstitions disguised in modern dress."

Real Discoveries

While the followers of Lamarck and Darwin were vainly endeavoring to find some convincing proof of the theory that new species can be evolved from existing ones, or at least that they were evolved in the past, an Augustinian Priest named Gregor Mendel (1822-1884), who was a contemporary of Darwin, was conducting scientific experiments for the purpose of producing new improved varieties of the same species, and he succeeded admirably. His success led to the discovery of the laws of heredity, and the production of improved varieties of cereals and improved breeds of the various domestic animals. It was Fr. Mendel's discovery that invalidated the theory of Darwin and forced evolutionists to abandon the original form and adopt a new theory which they called Neo-Darwinism. In an article in *The Catholic Encyclopaedia*, vol. 10, Sir Bertram Windle writes "Bateson in *Mendel's Principles of Heredity* claims that his (Mendel's) experiments are worthy to rank with those which laid the foundations of atomic laws of Chemistry and that this discovery was of importance very little inferior to those of a Newton or a Dalton."

Another discovery of lesser importance was made by Dr. Mivart who was an evolutionist and a contemporary of Darwin. It was to the effect that there are so many differences between the body of an ape and that of man, that it would be quite impossible to evolve the body of a man from an ape. This is now generally accepted by evolutionists who say that either the tarsier or the lemur was the common ancestor of man and ape. This retreat from Darwin's position increases that difficulty of finding a link between man and the lower animals.

Discovery Of The Fossil Remains Of Early Man

As it is conceded by Darwin and the evolutionists of his time, and by the evolutionists of our own time, including such men as the late Sir Julian Huxley, that the fossil remains of the various creatures that lived in this world, both animal and human, constitute the only direct proof of the evolution of either lower animal or man, an accurate knowledge of the fossil remains of the lower animals and especially of man is of paramount importance for the solution of the problem of the origin of species in general and of man in particular.

There was, first of all, the discovery of the fossils themselves, and this was made, for the most part, by chance, without the aid of organized expeditions, as in the case of the discoveries made in the ancient pre-flood cities. The discoveries of fossils claimed to be intermediary forms or missing links were practically all made by evolutionists and had not the testimony of independent witnesses. That part of the discovery did not take very long; in the few cases in which excavations were necessary, as in the case of the Peking Man at most it took only twenty years. But the most important part of the discovery, which was the discovery of the true facts about the men or the creatures to which the fossils belonged, in most cases, took from forty to a hundred years. In the cases of the fossils of the Neanderthal Man, which are by far the most important of all the fossils found since Darwin's time, this discovery took nearly a hundred years, and, in the meantime, they were used as evidence for the theory of the evolution of man by being represented in museums and in books as creatures more like apes than men.

The Fossils Discovered During Last Hundred Years

The Neanderthal Man

The first Neanderthal fossil discovered was a skull found at Gibraltar in 1848 but it attracted no attention at the time. The next was a skull found in Germany in the valley of the Neander river near Dusseldorf, in the year 1856. It was this skull that gave the Neanderthal name to the race to which it belonged. Later on, it was put forward by evolutionists as a skull of a "missing link" with a brain capacity of 230 cc. below the average for man. Forty years later, when several other Neanderthal skulls had been found, the skull was measured again and was found to be well above the average for modern man. When one erroneous statement was corrected, another was invented, which was, that the skull showed that the creature to which it belonged had its head bent forward like an ape's. Thirty years later, Professor Sergio Sergi, of the University of Rome, found a Neanderthal skull at Saccopastore, near Rome, which showed the Neanderthal skull was a normal human skull, and that the Neanderthal man walked perfectly erect. Then, in 1947, a discovery was made at Fontechevade in France by Mlle. Henri Martin, which showed that a race of men with skulls like those of modern man had existed in Europe before the arrival of the Neanderthal man. Finally, atheistic scientists who valued their reputation have written off the Neanderthal Man as a proof of evolution and classified him as a *Homo Sapiens*. In spite of all this, some Catholic evolutionists still use the Neanderthal man as a proof, not only of the theory of human evolution, but also of the theory of Polygenism.

The Dryopithecus

In 1856, a Frenchman named Edward Lartet found a mandible with a few teeth which, he thought, resembled human teeth, and claimed to have discovered "a missing link." In 1890, another Frenchman, named Gaudry, found a complete mandible in the same place, and pronounced it to be the mandible of an extinct species of monkey. Fossil teeth and several mandibles of different varieties of the same animal were later found in the Siwalik hills of India. There is no evidence that the creature to which the teeth and the mandibles belonged had any similarity to man, but evolutionists have given the creatures fancy names such as Bramepithecus, the Ramapithecus, etc., and have put them on their list of "missing links." They are on the list given by Fr. Francoeur in his *Perspectives in Evolution.*

The Pithecanthropus, Or Java Man

In 1889, Dr. Dubois, a Dutch surgeon, went to Java with the expectation of finding fossils of early man, which might be used as evidence for the theory of human evolution. Two years later he returned, bringing with him a quantity of fossils, all of which he concealed, except a thigh bone which he claimed to be human, and a skull, which he claimed to have a brain half-way between man's and ape's. As the brain-case of the skull had been removed, his claim for the sub-human brain capacity[1] could not be verified. When, after the lapse of thirty years, he produced the fossil he had concealed, the famous "Wadjak Skull" with a brain capacity of 1,700 cc. was found to be among them, Dr. Dubois admitted on more than one occasion before his death, that the first skull he produced belonged to a gibbon. Even if he had not made this admission, his claim to have found the fossil of a creature with sub-human brain capacity which

---

(1) For the reader who may not know it, the average brain-capacity of modern man's skull is about 1,500 cc, of woman about 1,350 cc; of male gorilla (which has the largest brain-capacity of animals) 600 cc; female less than 500 cc. No skull of any creature with a brain-capacity half-way between man and gorilla has ever been found.

walked erect would not be admitted in any court
of law. Three other attempts were made to find
"missing links" in Java, but they all ended in
failure.

The Piltdown Man

The Piltdown man was a case of pure fraud in
which leading English scientists were involved. In
1912, Charles Dawson, in an article in *The Man-
chester Guardian*, announced that a human skull
with a mandible in all respects like that of an ape,
except that the teeth were worn in the same manner as human teeth, had been found by men working in a gravel-pit at Piltdown. Subsequently a
number of primitive tools and the fossil bones of
various extinct animals were found in the same
place by Teilhard de Chardin, a French Jesuit
student, who was studying at the Jesuit College
at Hastings.

The claim was made by Dawson (who died in
1916) to have found a "missing link" was published in every country in the world and was used
by evolutionists for over forty years as evidence for
the theory of human evolution. In 1953, the truth
leaked out that the Piltdown man was a case of
forgery. Evolutionists became alarmed, and decided
to disown the Piltdown man, now that the facts
were known to a large number of people. Experts,
all of whom were evolutionists, were called in to
do the work of disowning. In the account of the
investigations made by them, which they published,
they admitted what was already known: that the

mandible, which was that of an ape, did not belong
to the skull, for the skull was several thousand
years old, while the mandible of the ape was a
fresh specimen only a few years old. The experts
admitted also that the mandible had been stained
to give the appearance of age, and that the teeth
had been filed to give them the appearance of
human teeth. The fraud consisted chiefly of re-
moving the human mandible and substituting the
ape's.

The Peking Man or Sinanthropus

The Peking Man, like the Piltdown Man, is a
case of fraud but of a different kind. The following
is a brief statement of the facts of the case:

After some preliminary investigation by various
experts which began as early as 1912, Dr. David-
son Black, an American surgeon, in 1926, obtained
a yearly grant of $20,000.00 from the Rockefeller
Institute for the purpose of carrying out excavations at a place called Chou-kou-tien, 37 miles from
Peking. He put a native Chinese, named Dr. Pei,
in charge of the excavation. Fossils or other objects of interest were to be brought to Peking for
examination. The excavations consisted in remov-
ing thousands of tons of limestone which had fallen
down from a limestone hill in a landslide that had
occurred thousands of years ago. When a portion
of the fallen limestone had been removed, beneath
it were discovered: (1) an enormous heap of ashes.
(2) thousands of dressed stones which had been
brought from a distance, presumably for the pur-

pose of constructing lime-kilns to burn the lime-stone, and (3) a number of skulls which probably were skulls of monkeys, because fossil skulls of monkeys were found in abundance in the district. Dr. Black selected one of the skulls found in the ashes to represent the Peking Man. Fr. Teilhard de Chardin, in an article in *Revue des Questions Scientifiques*, Paris, 1930, says that when the skull was found "the whole cerebral part was admirably preserved," but when Dr. Black exhibited the skull, the brain-case had been removed. Fr. Teilhard de Chardin invited his former professor, the famous Marcellin Boule, an evolutionist, but one of the world's greatest authorities on fossil skulls, to come out to China. Professor Boule came to China, but when he saw that the only proof which was pro-duced was a battered monkey's skull, he was very angry. He denounced Fr. de Chardin and poured ridicule on the claim that the creatures to which the battered skulls belonged could have carried on the large scale lime-burning industry which the excavations revealed. Professor Boule contended that the industry was evidently the work of real men. When Boule returned to France, Fr. Teilhard de Chardin began an article in which he attempted to refute Boule's statement, and to prove that there had been no real men about the place, but he left it unfinished until one day Dr. Pei brought in the fossil remains of ten real men, among which were three complete skulls. Fr. Teilhard finished the article at once, admitting that the fossils of real men had been found, but attempted to show that the real men whose fossils had been found had nothing to do with the industry. Fr. Teilhard's article was published in the *Revue des Questions Sc.* of 1934.

On the morning of the discovery of the fossils of real men, Dr. Black went into the laboratory to examine them, but *was found later on, lying dead among them.* It was Fr. Teilhard who first published the account of Dr. Black's death. Dr. Weidenreich was appointed by the Rockefeller Institute to succeed Dr. Black. Being evidently under the impression that no account of the discovery of the fossils of real men had been published, he decided to conceal the fact. He wrote an article in *Nature* in which he claimed that three more skulls of the Peking Man had been found, and that these skulls had a large brain capacity. Fr. Teilhard de Chardin wrote a new article, which he published in *Etudes.* In the article he denied what he had published in *Revue des Questions Sc.*, that fossils of real men had been found, and said that three more skulls of the Peking man, like the former, had been found. After the lapse of five years, Dr. Weidenreich published the true account; that the fossils of real men had been found; he published it first in China, a second time in a lecture at the university of California, and a third time in his book, *Apes, Giants and Men.*

From the above short summary of my thirty-page chapter in *Science of Today and the Problems of Genesis*, it should be abundantly clear that the first skull put forward by the late Dr. Black to represent the Peking Man was, as Professor Boule said, the skull of a monkey that had been killed and eaten by the workmen. Later, Dr. Weidenreich, who in his first article had concealed the fact that human skulls had been found, on three later occasions not only admitted the fact, but published photographs of them. The Peking Man is, therefore, a case of multiple fraud, or if you prefer, a pure myth for the fabrication of which $300,000 of good American money has been spent.

The Australopithecine Fossils

These fossils were found in South Africa, chiefly in the Transvaal, by Drs. Dart, Broom and Robinson at various times between 1925 and 1947. The three claims made for owners of these fossils: that they had a brain capacity of 750 cc.; that they manufactured primitive stone instruments, and that they knew the use of fire, have been rejected by authorities on palaeontology, such as Romer of America, and Boule and Vallois of France, who rejected outright the claims that the creatures made stone instruments and knew the use of fire, and put the brain capacity between 400 and 600 cc., which is the largest brain capacity of any animal. In *Evolution as a Process*, edited by the late Sir Julian Huxley, Sir S. Zuckerman has a fifty-page article on these fossils in which he proved that these are the fossils of animals which show no sign of evolution, and no similarity to man. Sir Julian Huxley, who accepts Zuckerman's solution, remarked that the case shows how cautious evolutionists should be before accepting claims made for newly-discovered fossils. However, practically all Catholic advocates of the theory of polygenism give these Australopithecine fossils among their proofs for a theory against the acceptance of which the Holy See has issued repeated warnings.

The Oreopithecus Fossils

These fossils were found in abundance near a coal mine in Baccinello in Northern Italy in 1870. A French palaeontologist named Gervais examined them in 1872, and gave his opinion that they belonged to an extinct species that resembled apes. A German palaeontologist named Schlosser, thought that they resembled fossils of baboons or long-tailed monkeys. In 1958 Dr. Hurzeler of Switzerland claimed that he had found fossils of the same creatures in the coal mine, but of this fact there is not sufficient evidence, and, as Hurzeler himself admitted, the fossils that he produced had no real resemblance to man.

The Zinjanthropus

In two articles in *The National Geographic Magazine*, in 1960 and 1961 Dr. Leakey, the author of *Adam's Ancestors*, informs his readers that the *National Geographic Society* had awarded him a "generous grant" (the amount of which he does not specify) for the purpose of exploring the Olduvai Gorge, in Tanganyika, with a view to writing some articles for their magazine. He had already explored the gorge to get material for *Adam's Ancestor's*, with results unfavourable to the theory of evolution, of which he was an ardent supporter.

On this occasion he found 400 fragments of what he claimed to be a *pre*-historic skull. He tells us that he attempted to reconstruct the skull, and find the brain-capacity, but he hinted that he did not expect his readers to take him seriously. In his *Adam's Ancestor*, he tells us that the workshops in which real men manufactured the instruments of the *Old Stone Age*, found all over Europe and Africa, had been discovered in this gorge. It may be presumed, therefore, that the four hundred splinters belong to the skull of a real man, and that Dr. Leakey's claim to have reconstructed the skull, need not be taken seriously.

Summary Of Conclusions

Geologists and archaeologists have provided us with the information that a great flood occurred at the end of the Ice Age about 7,000 B.C. which was caused by the subsidence of a great part of the Northern Hemisphere under the weight of ice and that the flood extended far beyond the area covered by the ice; that the human race must have been in that area because no trace of man has been discovered outside it; that Mesopotamia which, as we see, was the original home of the human race, was the first place to be inhabited after the flood; that before the dispersal after the Flood a hieroglyphic system of writing had been gradually developed which was brought by the Egyptians to Egypt, by the Chinese to China, and by the Indians to America; that before the flood, the common domestic animals—the ox, the sheep, the goat, and the pig and the horse—were kept, and the common cereals—wheat, barley and oats—were grown by earliest man; that household utensils, impliments of various kinds and weapons were developed from the first primitive attempts until they reached a high degree of perfection, and that soon before the Flood, tools and weapons were manufactured by hammering open-cast copper.

The evolutionists, who since Darwin's time have searched every part of the world in the hope of finding the fossils of intermediate forms between man and beast, have, by their failure to find even one such form, provided evidence that no such forms exist, and that no direct evidence can be found for the theory of evolution.

It can be claimed, therefore, that the great scientists of the past century have provided evidence in support of the biblical account of the origin of man, of the deluge, and of the manner of life of man from the earliest ages, both before and after the Flood; that they have provided evidence in support of the traditional teaching of the Church, that the human race is descended from one pair of ancestors, and hence that there is no need to alter the teaching of the Church about Original Sin.

The Arguments Used By The Catholic Authors Who Accept The Theory Of Polygenism

The Catholic authors who accept the theory of polygenism assert that modern scientific discoveries show that the present human population is not descended from a single pair of ancestors, but from several different pairs, and that the (alleged) discovery of the fact in modern times necessitates a change in the traditional explanation of the doctrine of original sin. They say that these conclusions follow from a proper understanding of the amended form of the theory of evolution called Neo-Darwinism, and from the discoveries of intermediate forms between man and the lower animal.

Now, in the first place, it must be noted that the same conclusions followed from the theory of evolution originally propounded by Darwin, but they were deliberately kept out of sight by Catholic propagandists for the theory of evolution at the beginning of the century, in order to avoid drawing upon themselves the censure of the Holy See.

The propagandists, especially those belonging to the Count Begouen circle of Toulouse in France, whose aim was to get the theory of evolution introduced into Catholic seminaries and colleges, discovered that the most effective form of propaganda was to concentrate on the "missing links"—the Neanderthal Man, etc.—as the most telling argument and to assert dogmatically that the theory which, they alleged, would ultimately have to be accepted by the Catholic Church, was in complete accord with the teaching of the Church and the biblical account of the creation of man, properly understood.

This insidious propaganda of the Count Begouen circle, which included men of influence like Canon Dorlodot of Louvain and Fr. Teilhard de Chardin, S.J., of France, succeeded too well, first in France, and then in other countries of Europe and America, with the result that the theory was accepted in many, if not most, of the Catholic seminaries and colleges of the world.

Now that the theory has got a firm foothold within the Catholic Church, and that the erroneous impression has been created that the arguments in favour of the theory of human evolution are so strong that they cannot be refuted, the propagandists have come out with the claim that the amended form of the theory of evolution called Neo-Darwinism involves the acceptance of the theory of polygenism (plurality of ancestors), which would make necessary a revision of the teaching of the Church about Original Sin.

Neo-Darwinism

As we have seen, Fr. Mendel's discovery of the principles of heredity rendered Darwin's original theory untenable, and forced his followers to amend it. The amended form is called Neo-Darwinism. Fr. Mendel produced new varieties of the same species, by crossing selected varieties of the same species and then by crossing the hybrids that resulted. Evolutionists attempted to produce new species by much the same method, but have failed to do so.

The first to make the experiment was Hugo de Vries, a Dutch botanist. He experimented in the American "evening primrose," and produced plants which he claimed to be new species. He attributed the change to the mutation in the genes and is known as the author of the "theory of Mutations."

It was discovered later on that the original plant that he was experimenting on was not a pure species, as he thought, but a hybrid, embodying characters from many varieties. These characters appeared in some of the daughter plants which, therefore, were not new species, but merely varieties of the same species. DeVries' experiment only verified Mendel's laws of heredity. T. H. Morgan carried out a number of experiments on the Drosophila Melanogaster (fruit fly). He bred up to 1,000 generations of them, but all were found to be different varieties of the fly, not a new species.

As these experiments only tended to demonstrate the present stability of the species, evolutionists gave as an excuse for the failure of the experiments, that at the end of the Pliocene Period, all the species had become "too highly specialized" and incapable of further evolution, but that before that period, evolution of species was produced by microscopic mutations continued over millions of years and directed by a force called Natural Selection, which they borrowed from Darwin's original system.

According to the present day exponents of Neo-Darwinism changes due to these microscopic mutations, have been taking place in whole groups of organisms simultaneously and whole new species of various kinds have been produced through the ages, but of that there is no proof.

Polygenism

The adherents of the theory of polygenism say that the human race must have been evolved in the same manner as the lower animals, and that unless God intervened by special miracle in favor of the human race, the present population of the world must be the descendants of many pairs of ancestors.

This is the first argument given for the theory of polygenism. The second argument is the alleged discovery during the past century in various part of the world, of a series of intermediate forms or "missing links."

Reply To The Main Arguments Of The Polygenists

(1) The theory of Neo-Darwinism has not been proved, and it is incapable of being proved.
(2) Each and every one of the fossils of intermediate form or "missing links" discovered during the century has been found on examination to be either the fossils of real men, as in the case of the Neanderthal Man, or the fossils of lower animals, as in the case of the Australopithicene fossils; no such thing as a fossil of a creature, half-man half-animal, has ever been found.

Now, with regard to the first point—the insuperable difficulties against Neo-Darwinism—Dr. Muller, who was awarded the Nobel Prize for his scientific experiments on the Drosophila Melanogaster fly, has very important evidence to give. He discovered that the exposure of an animal or plant to X-rays greatly increases the rate at which mutations appear; in the case of Drosophila Melanogaster, it was 15,000 per cent. This experiment was tried on this fly and other organisms but they were merely changed into different varieties of the same species, not into different species.

The late Sir Julian Huxley in *Evolution in Action* (page 47) refers to Dr. Muller's experiments and calculates the odds against a higher animal, such as a horse, being produced by chance mutation alone.

This he finds, to be one in a thousand raised to the millionth power, which would be represented by the figure 1 followed by a million naughts. Sir Julian adds:

"This is a meaningless large figure, but it shows what a degree of probability Natural Selection has to surmount and can surmount. . . .

"No one would bet on anything so improbable; and yet it has happened, thanks to the workings of Natural Selection."

The only definition that he can give of "natural selection" which can work such wonders is that it is *"a highly metaphorical term"* and he asks the following questions about what it can accomplish:

"Can it transform a reptile's scales into a bird's wing, or turn a monkey into a man?" "How can a blind automatic shifting process like mutation produce organs like the eye or the brain with their almost incredible complexity and delicacy of adjustment?"

"In a word, you are asking me to believe too much?"

The obvious answer is, of course, that a blind process like Natural Selection operating on another blind and undirected process, like mutation, could never possibly produce highly complicated organs like the eye or the brain, and that no person in possession of his senses should believe it could, but Sir Julian's answer is, that it is not too much to believe; that Natural Selection, working on rare chance mutations not only can produce, but actually has produced the eye and the brain.

If, as Sir Julian said, the original form of Darwinism was "an old superstition disguised in modern dress." Neo-Darwinism is another superstition a thousand times worse, and yet Catholic evolutionists not only accept this absurd system to explain the origin of lower animals, but also to explain the origin of man, which involves immeasurably greater improbability, and give it as one of the principal proofs of the theory of polygenism, which denies the unity of the human race and runs counter to the teaching of the Church about the doctrine of Original Sin.

The Second Argument

The second argument (sometimes put first) used in proof of the theory of polygenism is the alleged discovery of a number of intermediate forms, partly man, partly animal, in various parts of the world. This argument has been dealt with already by taking up one by one, these intermediate forms, of "missing links" put forward during the century and showing that the most important of them that had been used as evidence for the theory of evolution for more than a half-a-century have been discarded by prominent atheists, and that the remainder are all cases of fraud or error.

Argument From The Science Of Genetics

With regard to the claim by evolutionists that the origin of the various species now existing in the world can be explained by the science of genetics (which, as is admitted by biologists, is but a development of Mendelism), Douglas Dewar writes in *Man, a Special Creation* as follows: "Modern experimental work indicates that variations in organisms appear in consequence of (1) the duplication or multiplication of chromosomes that occur in the cell nucleus, (2) in the translocation or displacement of parts of chromosomes, (3) the loss of chromosomes or parts of chromosomes, (4) gene mutations which appear to be the result of the rearrangement of molecules that make up the gene, (5) loss of genes, (6) cross-breeding varieties.

"All the above causes are simply a shuffling or rearrangement of the chromosomes or of genes.

"Such rearrangement may be expected to yield a considerable amount of variation but clearly must be within type. . . ."[1]

(1) See appendix.

PART 2

The Catholic Advocates Of The Theory Of Polygenism

Catholic writers who openly advocate the theory of polygenism in books or articles constitute a very small group, but they appear to have a considerable following.

Fr. Francoeur, who advocates the theory, at least tentatively, mentions the names of the principal Catholic authors who advocate the theory, and bases his own arguments for the theory on their writings. Among these are Fr. Bone, S.J., of Louvain, Fr. Teilhard de Chardin, S.J., of France, from whose books he quotes at great length, and Frs. Schoonenberg and Smulders of Holland. In the French abridged edition of my larger work, *Science of Today and the Problems of Genesis*, I have dealt with the arguments for polygenism of Fr. Bone, S.J., and with the writings of Fr. Teilhard de Chardin on scientific subjects, and I find that in his book *Perspectives in Evolution*, Fr. Francoeur's main arguments for polygenism are substantially the same as those used by Fr. Bone, S.J., and that Fr. Teilhard de Chardin is his principal authority on scientific subjects.

Fr. Francoeur's "Perspectives In Evolution"

Fr. Francoeur devotes a major portion of his book to the discussion of the theory of polygenism and its relation to the doctrine of Original Sin. For his definition of evolution, he quotes with approval, the one given by a committee of fifty evolutionists at a convention held at the University of Chicago in 1959, which he sums up as follows:

"Two elements are vital in the definition: first, the acceptance of evolution as a scientifically established fact, and secondly, the application of that fact to all levels of observable definition."

In the Encyclical *Humani Generis* of Pope Pius XII, we read the direct contradiction of this definition:

"Some imprudently and indiscreetly hold that evolution, which has not been fully proved in the domain of natural sciences, explains the origin of all things, and audaciously support the monistic and pantheistic opinion that the world is in continual evolution. Communists gladly subscribe to this opinion."

We have already given reasons which show that the theory of evolution not only has not been proved, but has in fact collapsed.

On the question whether the present population of the world is descended from one pair of ancestors (monogenism) Fr. Francoeur says: "For the scientists, monogenism is very highly improbable and contrary to all the laws of nature as we know them today. Yet, we can always claim that God overrode the biological tendencies of nature. . . . Such extraneous interventions . . . seem unnecessary in the light of our knowledge of the created universe today."

From the above quotation it appears evident that Fr. Francoeur claims that the theory of human evolution is established in a form which excludes monogenism, and demands polygenism, but he admits the possibility of Divine intervention to prevent the effect of what he calls the "laws of nature." However, Pope Pius XII, of blessed memory, states categorically in the Encyclical *Humani Generis* that the theory of human evolution has not been proved, and in the same Encyclical he states: "The faithful cannot embrace that opinion which maintains either that after Adam there existed on earth true men who did not take their origin through natural generation from him as from the first parent of all, or that Adam represents a certain number of first parents."

Fr. Francoeur's Arguments For Evolution And Polygenism

Like all Catholic evolutionists, Fr. Francoeur endeavors to get rid of the testimony in the Bible in favor of the special creation of man. He does so as follows: "The author of Genesis did not give a second thought to the scientific details of the origin and structure of the universe. The details he needed for his story along these lines, he simply borrowed from the pagans. . . . This we must recognize as we read the accounts of man's origin." (op. cit. p. 162).

Fr. Francoeur's line of argument is: The Mosaic account of creation is not in agreement with the findings of science, therefore, we may ignore the Mosaic account of the origin of man. Now Professor Armellini, director of the Astronomical Observatory of Rome, stated in an article in *Studium*, 1946: "The Mosaic cosmogony is in perfect accord, indeed in amazing record, with the conclusions which modern astronomical cosmogony has reached."

The explanation of the origin of our planetary system and earth given by Fr. Francoeur (page 85), which is a modification of the Laplace theory, that the earth and the planets have been formed from the same nebulae as the sun, has been proved to be no longer tenable by the discovery that the sun is composed of 99% hydrogen gas and contains only 1% of the elements of the earth. (See *The Nature of the Universe* by F. Hoyle, page 33).

After his abortive attempt to explain the origin of the universe, Fr. Francoeur proceeds to explain the origin of life and of all living things. On page 89 he says: "Thus the origin of life, as suggested in 1924 by Oparin, a Russian scientist, has been confirmed." Fr. Francoeur refers to experiments from which amino acids and sugars are produced, but this is a long way off from the production of the first living cell. Fr. Francoeur continues: "We have no evidence either direct or indirect of the earliest forms of life. . . . However, we can *theorize* about the stages that must have occurred during that tedious evolution."

This is a significant admission; that no direct evidence can be produced, either for the origin of life, or the early forms of life, Darwin makes the same admission, and makes no attempt to fill the void, but Fr. Francoeur gives an imaginary account of primitive forms that must have existed hundreds of millions of years before the Cambrian Period if the theory of evolution is true, but of which no trace has been found.

The Cambrian Period

In the 10th chapter of *The Origin of Species*, Darwin admits, and Fr. Francoeur and all evolutionists have to admit, that myriads of fossils of all species, genera, families, orders, classes and phyla of the invertebrates suddenly appear in the sedimentary rocks of the Cambrian Period. There were sedimentary rocks before the Cambrian Period —rocks formed from the sediment at the bottom of the ocean, brought from dry land by the rivers— but they contained no fossils. There is no satisfactory explanation for the sudden appearance of fossils of myriads of perfectly formed creatures of innumerable varieties, except that they were created directly by Almighty God.

Between the Cambrian Period and the present day, the various classes, orders, families, genera,

and species of living things, have appeared suddenly at intervals. Even evolutionists are forced to
admit that, so far, no link between the invertebrates
and the vertebrates has been found, nor has any
link between the various classes, orders and families been found. Most of those who hold that living
things were originally created or formed directly by
God are willing to admit that the family was the
unit of creation, though that is by no means certain. However, Fr. Francoeur gives an account of
the origin of the various phyla, orders, families,
genera and species by evolution, ascribing each to
the period in which fossils suddenly appeared, as
if it were certain that their origin was by evolution
and not by special creation and this is made the
prelude to his account of the origin of man by
evolution.

Fr. Francoeur's Account Of The Origin Of Man

At the time that Fr. Francoeur was writing, Darwin's theory that man was descended from the ape
was universally rejected by evolutionists as being
biologically impossible. He, therefore, gives the
present-day form of the theory, that man and ape
has a common ancestor. Evolutionists are divided
in their choice of a common ancestor, between the
lemur and the tarsier; Fr. Francoeur chooses the
tarsier.

The same objection can be made against the
lemur and the tarsier as against Darwin's ape, that

they are too highly specialized, and the difficulty in establishing a genetic link between either the lemur or the tarsier and man is many times greater than in establishing a link between the ape and man.

There is nothing original about Fr. Francoeur's attempt to establish a link; he just gives the conventional list of "missing links" found in books by evolutionists of the last twenty years, and adds Hurzeler's Oreopithecus and Leakey's Zinjanthropus, which are not taken seriously by leading authorities on human fossils.

Atheists with a reputation to maintain like the late Sir Julian Huxley of England, or Boule and Vallois of France, will not hesitate about discarding from their list of "missing links" any that is not genuine; Marcellin Boule rejected the Peking Man with scorn; Vallois admitted that the Neanderthal Man was a normal man with prominent eye-brows; Julian Huxley rejected the Australopithecine fossils of the Transvaal, but Catholic evolutionists like Fr. Francoeur, keep them all on their list, and they do so where Catholic doctrine is at stake. Everybody now knows and admits that the pagan dieties, such as Jupiter and Venus, had no real existence, but were just mythical beings, and yet many early Christians were put to death for refusing to offer incense to them; the "missing links" given by Fr. Francoeur never had any real existence, no more than the pagan deities, and yet they are used by Fr. Francoeur and his associates in an endeavor to show that the teaching of the Church on Original Sin requires to be modified.

Fr. Teilhard De Chardin, S.J.

Fr. Francoeur devotes a large portion of his book to the late Fr. Teilhard de Chardin and his writings; he puts him among the greatest scientists of our age, and in addition, he refers to him as a mystic, theologian and philosopher. He is Fr. Francoeur's chief authority on the questions he discusses, and it would appear from his references to him, that Fr. Francoeur regards his opinion on the questions at issue of greater weight than the combined opinions of all the Popes of the last century. The idea that Fr. Teilhard is one of the greatest scientists of our age, who has succeeded in reconciling the doctrines of Christianity with the findings of modern science where others have failed is an opinion that is accepted by practically all evolutionists, and has been made an important part of the propaganda for the diffusion of the theory of evolution inside of the Catholic Church for the past half-century but this opinion is by no means universally accepted. A large part of the popularity which his books enjoy inside the Church is due to the writings of a few Jesuit Fathers and laymen, who carried on correspondence with him during his lifetime, some as long as thirty years, while he was composing his books, and who, therefore, are partly responsible for their contents. Chief among these men are Fr. de Lubac, S.J., who corresponded with him for thirty years, and Claude Cuenot, his biographer. These men, in defending Fr. Teihard, are really defending themselves.

A very different picture of Fr. Teilhard de Chardin and his writings is to be got from the pronouncements of the Holy See against his writings, which forbid their sale in Catholic book shops, forbid students of ecclesiastical colleges to read them; which declare that they contain grave errors against the faith and that they are full of ambiguities. The Holy See and Fr. Teilhard's religious superiors intervened no less than seven times in an endeavour to prevent the poison contained in these books from being spread all over the world.

In Fr. Teilhard's own country, France, prominent theologians, like Fr. Philip of the Trinity O.D.C., one of the Consultors of Vatican II, has analysed his religious writings and pointed out the grave errors against the faith which they contain and prominent scientists like Professors Bounoure and Vernet of France have done the same for his scientific writings and have shown that he has no claim to be called a great scientist, or even to be called a scientist at all, but that he should rather be classified among the theosophists.

In particular, they show that all he has written about the intermediate forms called "missing links" which he has represented as genuine, has been found to be cases either of fraud or error. His articles on the fossil remains of man, and any other articles that had any claim to be called scientific, were all published during his lifetime with the permission of his superiors, who refused permission for the publication of his two main works, *The Phenomenon of Man*, and *Le Milieu Divin, because they contained grave errors against the faith.*

Fr. Teilhard De Chardin Very Much Misrepresented

For the most of the clergy and laity, Fr. Teilhard de Chardin is an enigma: on the one hand, the Holy See has issued repeated warnings against his writings, one of which declared that they contained grave errors against the faith, and were dangerous, especially for the young; on the other hand, some Catholic authors with reputations for learning have praised the books without reserve, not only for their scientific contents but also for their treatment of the religious life, and as the result of these recommendations, the books have found their way into the convents in different countries and have been read eagerly by some of the Sisters.

Now, as a contemporary of Fr. Teilhard, and as a missionary who was in China for over twenty years at the same time as Fr. Teilhard, and who has carried out exhaustive research work on the problems that he has dealt with, I venture to give the following facts about him that are not generally known and which, I believe, will go a long way toward explaining the grave errors against the faith, and the origin of the peculiar ideas about the worship of nature to be found in his writings:

The period of his childhood, youth and early manhood was a period of intense atheistic propaganda in France during which the Catholic Church was being persecuted by the Masonic Government in power. The Religious Orders, male and female, were driven out of the schools and hospitals all over France, and their property was confiscated.

It was a period also during which the heresy of Modernism, which was condemned by Pope St. Pius X, was rampant in France.

An indication that the Teilhard family may have come under the influence of the subversive ideas of the time may be found in the following incident related about Teilhard as a child of six by Miss Hilda Graef in her short life of him. In her book *Mystics of Our Time*, she tells that as a child of six, when he might be expected to be lisping the Hail Mary, that he used to say, "God, Iron" and that his commentary on this childish habit sixty years later was: "In this instinctive movement which made me truly worship a small piece of metal, there was a strong sense of self-giving, mixed up with a whole train of obligations, and my spiritual life has been merely a development of this." Fr. North confirms Miss Graef's account of young Teilhard adoring a piece of iron and adds that his mother, who was a pious woman, was a relative of Voltaire. (See *Teilhard and the Creation of the Human Soul* by Fr. North.)

While still a Jesuit student, he became a member of the Count Begouen circle at Toulouse, the object of which was to propagate Darwin's theory in France and to introduce it into the Catholic seminaries, and he became the most extreme and active propagandist among the members. When he went to the Jesuit College at Hastings in England, he made the acquaintance of the small group of men who were engaged in promoting what is now known as the Piltdown Man forgery. He was even then under the erroneous impression that several "missing links" had been found and readily accepted the promoters' account of the forgery that another link between man and beast had been discovered. Fr. Teilhard began to pay frequent visits to the gravel pit where the fossils were said to have been found, and when the conspirators in the forgery learned this they instructed the workmen to allow him to pick up these objects as they were dug, and they paid the workmen a substantial gratuity for each flint or bone that Fr. Teilhard brought to them. (See *The Piltdown Forgery*, by J. G. Weiner, London, 1955.) All the objects planted including the ape's jawbone, passed through his hands; however, in the five years during which he had been visiting the scene of the forgery, he discovered nothing wrong and he continued to use the Piltdown Man for forty years (after which the forgery was admitted) as a proof of human evolution.

The Peking Man

I have already given an account of the case of the Peking Man and of the part which Fr. Teilhard played in it. The sole fact that Dr. Marcellin Boule, the greatest authority of his time on human fossils, Fr. Teilhard's former professor and friend, a lifelong propagandist of the theory of evolution, who travelled out to China prepared to support the new "missing link," saw himself forced to reject it because there was not even a *prima facie* case, should be sufficient evidence for any unbiased person, that the Peking Man was another case of forgery.

Evidence has come to light which shows the extreme simplicity and credulity of Fr. Teilhard. The fossil skull of the monkey from which the brain-case had been removed that was presented to Marcellin Boule as evidence and rejected by him, and the fossil remains of real men subsequently found in the excavations, which showed that Boule was right, have disappeared. These, if they could be found, would provide additional evidence that the Peking Man was another case of forgery. Now it appears that Fr. Teilhard did his best to preserve them. His secretary, a German lady, is alleged to have stated that Fr. Teilhard entrusted these fossils to her, and that she put them on board an American ship, after the Japanese had surrendered, but that they "disappeared." A letter published in a New York newspaper which was signed by an American member of the crew of the ship stated that the fossils were put on board but that they disappeared. The sailor in question did not say how.

But the circumstances which, most probably, was responsible for the views expressed in his principal work, *The Phenomenon of Man* was his post-graduate course in philosophy at the Sorbonne University, Paris. At the time that he studied there, the system of philosophy taught was the system of Auguste Comte, positivism, a system which recognizes only positive and observable phenomena.[1] Fr. Teilhard's phenomenology is only another name for positivism, while he protests in *The Phenomenon of Man* that he is treating only the phenomena

(1) See *The Future of Man,* Chapter X, in which Fr. Teilhard refers to Professors Durkeim and Levy-Bruhl, two of Comte's most famous disciples who were in the Sorbonne when Teilhard was there.

in man that can be observed by the senses, he invades both the metaphysical and the supernatural domains.

Fr. Francoeur dissects the book for his readers and lays bare the absurdities which friends of Fr. Teilhard, like Fr. Lubac, try to conceal. The following is a brief outline of the book, which can be verified by reading either the book itself or Fr. Francoeur's Chapter IV, which gives Fr. Teilhard's views with substantial accuracy:

All matter has a "within" and a "without." The "within" of matter is consciousness. Consciousness increases according as matter become more complex, and the increase goes on until consciousness reaches what Fr. Teilhard calls the "boiling point" when life is born (this is spontaneous generation). Simultaneously with the birth of life there is formed around the earth, just above the atmosphere, another sphere which Fr. Teilhard calls the "biosphere." Life goes on evolving and the biosphere goes on developing until a new "boiling point" is arrived at when life becomes conscious of itself in some of the higher animals that have concentrated their energy in evolving bigger brains, and thus, thought is generated, and the higher animal becomes a man. Fr. Francoeur describes the birth of man as follows: "As the irrational primate stems converged some twenty million years ago, a new critical threshold was reached, a boiling point, and man emerged."

While this was going on, a new sphere was being formed around the earth above the biosphere, which Fr. Teilhard calls the noosphere (the sphere of mind). On page 151 of *The Future of Man*, Fr. Teilhard himself describes the noosphere as "an actual layer of vitalized substance, outside and above the biosphere enveloping the earth."

Towards the end of the book, Fr. Teilhard mentions the name of God for the first time, and endeavours to fit in Christ and Christianity into his irrational and absurd system.

In the course of the book Fr. Teilhard comes down to earth occasionally with some scientific information in an attempt to provide a scientific basis for his theories, but in every case without exception his scientific information is out of date. For instance, to explain the origin of our earth, he gives a modified form of the Laplace theory, which says that the earth was formed from the sun. It is now known with certainty that the sun is composed of 99% hydrogen gas, and that it would be impossible to form the earth from it. Then in order to explain the origin of man from a lower animal, he gives the conventional list of "missing links," all of which have been proved to be cases of fraud or error, as I have already shown.

Some French scientists contend that *The Phenomenon of Man* should be classified among books on theosophy, and Fr. Teilhard himself among theosophists. Theosophy in its modern form is defined by the Oxford Dictionary as "a system of speculation which claims a knowledge of nature more profound than can be obtained from empirical science. . . ." Fr. Teilhard speaks of inanimate matter having "consciousness"; the consciousness reaching a "boiling point" and producing life; this life evolving into different forms and producing thought and giving birth to man, while at the same time two new spheres of real substance—the biosphere and the noosphere—are being produced. For all this he gives no proof whatsoever and yet he speaks with as much assurance and as dogmatically as if he had special revelation from Almighty God.

It is in favor of this tissue of absurdities that Fr. Francoeur, and the authors from whom he quotes as sharing his views about Fr. Teilhard, reject the Mosaic account of creation, which has God as its Author, and advocate the theory of polygenism and a revision of the teaching of the doctrine of the Church on Original Sin.

"Teilhard And The Creation Of The Human Soul"

by

Fr. Robert North, S.J.

Fr. North's book is based on several false assumptions. (1) IIc represents Fr. Teilhard as a great scientist and in particular as an eminent palaeontologist. The facts are that Fr. Teilhard had little interest in science except insofar as it provided a basis for his extreme theory of evolution; his chief interest was in the system of philosophy of Auguste Comte which he studied at the Sorbonne University, Paris, under Comte's most famous disciples. (2) Fr. North assumes that the theory of evolution, even as applied to explain the origin of the human body, is now firmly established and that opposition to it has now almost ceased. The facts are that the main argument for evolution, which is the existence of fossils of intermediate forms (as is admitted by Darwin, Julian Huxley, etc.) has collapsed completely, and that opposition to the theory is steadily growing in America and is very much in evidence in France, Spain and Italy. (3) He assumes that the attitude of the Holy See towards the theory that man's body was derived from that of a lower animal has changed, and on p. 37 states in proof of that assertion

> "Since 1890 numerous Catholic authorities have been maintaining that *bodily* evolution is not incompatible with our faith in Scriptural revelation. . . . In fact by 1950 so many Catholic theologians had orally or guardedly adhered to this view that its authorization in *Humani Generis* merely made officially legitimate what was already the consensus of experts."

And on page 64 Fr. North states:

> "Many Catholics were among these (who believed in evolution) even before it was officially decreed in 1950 that bodily evolution is not incompatible with Church teaching."

Fr. North grossly misrepresents the teaching of *Humani Generis* on the theory of evolution. It is nowhere stated in this Encyclical that "bodily evolution is not incompatible with Church teaching" as the following quotations from *Humani Generis* will show:

"Some imprudently and indiscreetly hold that evolution, *which has not been fully proved even in the domain of natural sciences*, explains the origin of all things, and audaciously support a monistic and pantheistic opinion that the world is in continual evolution. Communists gladly subscribe to this opinion. . . ."

". . . The teaching authority of the Church does not forbid that, in conformity with the present state of human science and sacred theology, research and discussion on the part of men experienced in both fields take place with regard to the theory of evolution in as far as it inquires into the origin of the human body as coming from pre-existent and living matter. . . ."

"Some rashly transgress this liberty of discussion when they act as if the origin of the human body from pre-existing and living matter were already completely certain and proved by the facts that have been discovered up to now. . . ."

From these quotations it can be clearly seen: (a) that the extreme form of evolution taught in Fr. Teilhard's *The Phenomenon of Man* is rejected outright; (b) that nothing more than *discussion* about the possibility of evolution of man from pre-existing living matter is permitted; (c) that this permission for discussion (which was already going on without restriction) is now restricted to experts "in the human sciences and sacred theology;" (d) that all Catholics, including the experts in both fields, are forbidden to teach the evolution of man's body from a lower animal as an established fact.

It is stated in an earlier part of *Humani Generis* that this Encyclical, like other Papal Encyclicals, binds in conscience.

There has never been any declaration by the Holy See that the theory of the origin of man's body from a lower animal can be reconciled with the teaching of the Church, nor is there any consensus of opinion among theologians on that point. Fr. Sagues, S.J., (to whom Fr. North refers several times) in Vol. II of *Sacrae Theologiae Summa* states and gives proof of the thesis, that the theory known as "mitigated evolution" cannot be reconciled with the teaching of the Church, and he received a letter of commendation written by the present Pope Paul VI (when he was substitute Secretary of State) on behalf of Pope Pius XII when this volume was presented to His Holiness.

(4) Fr. North wrongly assumes that as the result of recent discoveries, the theory of evolution both as applied to species in general and to man in particular, is now practically certain and that opposition to it, at least inside the Catholic Church, has ceased. Fr. North could not be further from the truth. In 1950 Pope Pius XII was able to state confidently that the theory of evolution had not up to then been proved. The case of evolution has worsened since then. It was after 1950 that the argument based on the fossil (which is the only direct argument) collapsed. The collapse began with the discovery in 1953 that the case of the Piltdown Man was a case of pure fraud in which prominent English scientists were involved. Fr. Teilhard was a frequent visitor to Piltdown during the five

years he spent at the Jesuit College of Hastings and for forty years continued to believe that the Piltdown Man was a genuine "missing link." The collapse continued and now it is complete. Neither Fr. North nor all the authorities that he quotes could now defend one single case of "missing link" or intermediate form from all the cases that had been put forward since the time of Darwin.

The Main Thesis Of Fr. North's Book

On page 164, Fr. North writes:

> "Of all the threshold leaps (in the process of evolution) attested in the evolving reality around us, none is so exciting and so baffling, even for the scientist, as the emergence of the human spirit. . . ."

> "Teilhard explicitly spelled out *in several footnotes* (italic type mine) the appropriateness of linking these natural observations with what Revelation teaches about the immediate creation of the soul by God."

On this point there seems to be a radical difference of opinion between Fr. North and Fr. Francoeur. Fr. North bases his defense of Fr. Teilhard's orthodoxy about the origin of the human soul on a number of footnotes in *The Phenomenon of Man;* Fr. Francoeur ignores the footnotes and gives his summary of Fr. Teilhard's account of the origin of man (including the human soul) as follows:

"As the irrational primate stems converged some twenty million years ago, a new critical threshold was reached, a "boiling point" and man emerged." *Perspectives in Evolution*, p. 140.)

Now the question arises, what guarantee has Fr. North that the footnotes are the work of Fr. Teilhard himself? The Very Rev. Fr. Arrupe, the newly-elected General of Jesuits, at his first press conference, cast doubts on the fidelity of the text of Fr. Teilhard's works to what was written by him. All of Fr. Teilhard's manuscripts were given to Mlle. Mortier, of Paris; the Jesuit Fathers had no control over them and could not prevent them from being tampered with.

A further question arises: why were these manuscripts not given to Fr. de Lubac, S.J., who, according to his own statements in *La Pensee Religieuse du Pere Teilhard de Chardin* (p. 17) carried on correspondence with him for thirty years and had a long interview with him in 1954, a few months before his death? Or to some of the other Jesuit Fathers mentioned by Fr. Lubac? Fr. Teilhard de Chardin appointed the late Sir Julian Huxley and Professor Gaylord Simpson, two militant atheists, among his literary executors, but no Jesuit Father; after his death an international committee composed mostly of atheists took over Fr. Teilhard's manuscripts from Mlle. Mortier and published them without the permission of the General of the Jesuits and without *imprimatur*. The Jesuits get no share in the immense profits made by the sale of these works; atheists like Sir Julian Huxley have used them for the propagation of atheism; Russian Communists have translated into Russian. Would it not, therefore, be more fitting for Fr. Teilhard's friends among the Jesuit Fathers to appoint a day of mourning, to be observed each year, over a member of the Society of Jesus who has been used after his death by atheists and Communists to propagate their nefarious doctrines; and a day of prayer for the repose of his soul, than to be using his name as a peg on which to hang their own views, in defiance of the wishes of the Holy See? If Fr. de Lubac or Fr. North, or any other of Fr. Teilhard's brethren, think they have some message to communicate to the public let them write it in their own name and sign it and allow Fr. Teilhard to rest in peace.

On page 40 Fr. North makes a show of impartiality when he writes: "Teilhard clearly and vigorously indicates that his own sympathies . . . lie with polygenism" and quotes from his writings to show that this is true.

On page 6, he gives a short quotation, out of its context, from a reply to a letter received from a Dominican Father who had left the Church, inviting Fr. Teilhard to do likewise and to join him in founding a new sect. By his reference to this letter Fr. North shows that he is aware of its existence but he gives no idea of its contents; why does he not give the contents of this letter?

The following quotations from this letter, which is given in full in the brochure by Henri Rambaud will show that Fr. Teilhard aimed at nothing less than bringing about a radical change in the teaching of the Catholic Church:

> "Basically I consider—as you do—that the Church (like any living reality after a certain time) reaches a period of mutation or necessary reformation. . . . To be more precise, I consider that the reformation in question(much more profound a one than that of the 16th century) [the Protestant Reformation] is no longer a simple matter of institutions and ethics but one of faith. . . .

> "Having stated my views, I still cannot see any better means of bringing about what I anticipate than to work towards the reformation (as defined above) from within. . . .

> "In the course of the last fifty years I have watched the revitalization of Catholic thought and life taking place around me—in spite of the Encyclicals—too closely not to have unbounded confidence in the ability of the old Roman stem to revivify itself. Let us work each in our separate spheres. All upward movements converge.

> Yours sincerely,
> Teilhard de Chardin."

The reformation which Fr. Teilhard advocated was more profound than that effected in the Protestant Reformation of the Sixteenth Century; he wanted to have removed articles of faith which the Sixteenth Century: reformers retained. Teilhardism is therefore, just as much opposed to that form of Protestantism which retains the doctrines taught in the Bible and expressly accepted by the reformers, as it is to Catholicism, and if permitted by the Magisterium of the Catholic Church, would be an insuperable obstacle to the reunion of Christendom. The Magisterium of the Catholic Church has emphatically rejected Teilhardism: In 1957 the Congregation of the Holy Office forbade the sale of Fr. Teihard's books in all Catholic book shops and ordered them to be removed from all libraries of all ecclesiastical seminaries and religious houses; in 1962 the some congregation issued a *monitum* with the approval of Pope John XXIII in which it was stated that these writings contained grave errors against the Faith. This *monitum* was published in *L'Osservatore Romano* of July, 1962, and in the same issue was published an article giving a list of the principal errors contained in the writings of Fr. Teilhard which include errors about the teaching of the Church on creation, on Christ, on the Incarnation and Redemption, on spirit and matter, and on Original Sin; and in September of 1966 the Congregation for the Doctrine of the Faith declared that the *monitum* issued in 1962 is still in force.

Fr. North appears to have doubts about the propriety of recommending the writings of Fr. Teilhard to Catholics and calls to his aid Fr. Rahner, S.J. Fr. Rahner contributes an introduction to Fr. North's book in which he states: "If I offer a recommendation along with this . . . book, it is neither my intention nor the author's that we should divide responsibility for the views put forward." However, he does recommend the book.

Chapter 8 of the book has the heading "Rahner's Hypothesis of Hominization" and is taken from the book entitled *Hominization* which Fr. North tells us "is coauthored by Fr. Rahner, S.J., and Fr. Paul Overhage, S.J." and that "the part signed by Rahner maintains expressly that the immediate creation of every human soul out of nothing is a Catholic Dogma." Fr. Rahner seeks to save his own reputation as a theologian, and at the same time he associates himself with a defense of Fr. Teilhard's theory of the origin of the human soul. Fr. Rahner is coauthor with Fr. Overhage, S.J., of *Hominization*, a book which assumes the evolution of the human body. When Fr. Rahner contributes an introduction to Fr. North's book and is coauthor with Fr. Overhage, S.J., of *Hominization*, he cannot by a mere declaration free himself from the responsibility of defending Fr. Teilhard's account of the origin of the human soul and Fr. Overhage's defense of the theory of human evolution which is based on the alleged existence of a series of hominids which never really existed.

Many excuses can be made for Fr. Teilhard. He was not one of the authors of Modernism, but was a victim of those errors; he has incorporated them in his writings and these writings are being used to propagate a form of Modernism more insidious than that condemned by Pope St. Pius X; he was not the author of the theory of human evolution, but imbibed the theory in his youth and having become a believer in it, and being simple and credulous, was made a common fool of at Piltdown and at Choukou-tien in China; he did not invent the

theory of positivism or its modern form, phenomenology, but being a man totally devoid of the critical faculty that discovers error under disguise,
imbibed the theory at the Sorbonne University
from the disciples of August Comte.

The same excuses cannot be made for those
writers who claim to be men of critical judgment
and were not exposed to the temptations to which
Fr. Teilhard succumbed.

Teilhard De Chardin's Theology Of The Christian In The World

by
Fr. Robert L. Faricy, S.J.

Fr. Faricy dedicates his book to Mlle. Jeanne
Mortier, who, he says, "has done so much for the
Church in making known the ideas of Fr. Teilhard
de Chardin." By dedicating his book to Mlle.
Mortier, Fr. Faricy condemns it in advance and
condemns himself and Fr. Teilhard as well, for the
service with Mlle. Mortier rendered to the Church
was to get hold of the mss. of Fr. Teilhard, containing his writings which had already been refused
permission for publication by his Jesuit Superiors
and by the Holy See, and, after his death, to pub-
lish them in defiance of the wishes of the Jesuit
Superiors and the Holy See.

Fr. Faricy makes no mention of the fact that
the Holy See had intervened several times to prevent the publication of Fr. Teilhard's writings,
both before and after his death.

An account of these interventions by the Holy See has already been given; also of the letter in *L'Osservatore Romano*, of June, 1962, with a list of the principal errors in the writings of Fr. Teilhard.

Fr. Faricy states in the preface of his book that its purpose was "neither to attack nor to defend Teilhard's general perspectives or any of his ideas, but simply to set forth a coherent summary of his views." While making no mention of the article in *L'Osservatore* (of June 30th, 1962) Fr. Faricy in the course of his book, includes all the errors mentioned in this article and many more, so that his book might be regarded as an exposure of the fundamental errors contained in Fr. Teilhard's writings and a justification of the action taken by the Holy See under several Popes to warn the faithful against them. Fr. Faricy's book consists, in large measure, of quotations from the writings of Fr. Teilhard, many of which are the same as those given in *L'Osservatore Romano* in which the errors referred to are contained.

Fr. Faricy's attempt to construct "a theology of the Christian" from these quotations is as futile as would be an attempt to build a cathedral on a swamp from the refuse dumped there from a neighboring city.

Fr. Teilhard's "Mass On The World"

Fr. Faricy includes an account of Fr. Teilhard's "Mass on the World" about which his supporters are divided. Some of them, among whom is the late

Sir Julian Huxley, former leader of the English atheists, refer to it with admiration while others are scandalized. This "Mass on the World" is not a Mass at all in the usual sense, but a series of reflections on the Mass with which most Catholics do not agree. Fr. Teilhard's superior to whom he sent the manuscript containing these reflections was alarmed because he thought they were capable of a pantheistic interpretation.

The account of "the Mass on the World" is taken from Teilhard's book (or collection) called *The Hymn of the Universe*. In this book Teilhard describes a number of "experiences" (whether real or imaginary is not clear) in which he saw the Host expanding and embracing the world. As the result of these experiences he says:

"My spirit has always naturally pantheistic. I felt its inborn an unconquerable aspirations, but I dare not give them free rein because I could not reconcile them with my faith. *After these experiences, and others like them* I have found a life-long unexhausted interest and an unalterable peace. I live in the heart of a single element, the centre and the detail of all-personal love and cosmic power."

The Foundation Of Fr. Teilhard's New Religion

Fr. Teilhard makes evolution the foundation of his "Theology of the Christian."

"Evolution," he says, "is not just hypothesis or a theory. . . . It is a general condition to which all theories, all hypotheses, all systems must bow and which they must satisfy if they are thinkable and true."

Evolution is only a theory; after a hundred years' research no proof that the origin of the various species of living things can be explained by the theory of evolution has been found, and in the case of man, all attempts to find a link between him and the lower animals have failed completely. What evolutionists call "the machinery of evolution" (or the forces that produce it) which Fr. Teilhard uses is not based on phenomena that can be observed, as he claims. The force to which he appeals is called by him "the within" of things; this is a mysterious force for which he enacts a law which he calls "the law of Complexity-consciousness." By means of this mysterious force operating according to an imaginary law he gets life spontaneously generated in the brute beasts, and then he gets thought and with it the human soul generated, so that a lower animal becomes a man. Fr. Faricy says expressly that he merely gives Fr. Teilhard's views but does not defend them; on page 164 of *Teilhard and the Creation of the Human Soul* Fr. North implies the same thing, when he defends the footnotes of *The Phenomenon of Man* only, and makes no mention of the text. In a footnote to page 95 Fr. Faricy gives the following quotation from Professor Simpson of Hartford University (whom Fr. Teilhard appointed as one of his literary executors):

"Teilhard's beliefs as to the couse and causes of evolution are not scientifically acceptable be-

cause they are not based on scientific premises."
Simpson is an extreme evolutionist and being one
of Fr. Teilhard's literary executors would have de-
fended him if he could have done so without loss
to his own reputation.

*Origin of Fr. Teilhard's delusion that brute mat-
ter (matter without life or soul usually called inert
matter) had a "within."*

Fr. Robert North, S.J., appears to think that Fr.
Teilhard borrowed the idea that brute matter contained consciousness, from Bergson's *Creative Edu-
cation*; Miss Hilda Graef thinks it is a form of panpsychism. In her *Mystics of Our Time* (p. 234)
she says: "This is a hypothesis unacceptable to
most scientists as well as theologians, because it
endows with a 'soul' beings which neither of them
can admit to have. Indeed, this poetic concept re-
sembles a kind of panpsychism which was formerly
rejected by St. Thomas Aquinas." From the evidence available however, the most probable explanation of the origin of the erroneous idea seems to
be that he imbibed it as a child from someone who
had great influence over him. Several of his admirers tell how he used to "adore" a piece of iron
as a child of six and endeavour to interpret it as
a favourable omen. Fr. Robert North says: "IIis
'adoring' the lump of iron is the clue to an essen-
tially God-seeking satisfaction." (op. cit. p. 2) Another of his admirers says that his mother took
the piece of iron from him and, when he cried to
get it back, consoled him by explaining to him the
love of the Sacred Heart. If she did so, she did
not convince him, for more than sixty years later,

he wrote: "In this instinctive movement which made me truly worship a small piece of metal, there was a strong sense of self-giving mixed up with a whole train of obligations, and *my whole spiritual life has merely been a development of this.*" (*Mystics of Our Time*, p. 218.)

The incident of adoring a piece of iron as a child and the fact that he clung to the belief all his life that inert matter has "a within" which made it in some way worthy of worship, is an indication that he was abnormally credulous as a child and remained so all his life. This appears from the way he allowed himself to be fooled by the conspirators who concocted the Piltdown Man fraud in England and afterwards by those who concocted the Peking Man fraud in China. Miss Hilda Graef relates the following incident in connection with the Peking Man excavations: At one stage of the excavations, when Dr. Black, the chief conspirator, was confident that he had established his claim of having discovered the fossil of a new primitive creature half-ape and half-man that knew the use of fire, the fossil bones of a number of real men were found in the same place and brought into his laboratory in Peking. Dr. Black went to examine them and *was subsequently found dead among them.* Fr. Teilhard, instead of waking up to the fact that the Peking Man was a hoax and of seeing in the sudden death of Dr. Black at least a warning to have nothing further to do with the case, took an oath over Dr. Black's dead body "to struggle harder than ever to give hope to man's labour and research." "He felt that no human effort could be of any avail unless there is some natural as well as supernatural future for the universe in the direction of some kind of immortal consciousness." (p. 230 *Mystics of Our Time*.)

Both Fr. North, S.J., and Miss Hilda Graef give Fr. Teilhard's views about the efforts of missionaries to convert such people as the Indians and Chinese. They were, to quote from Miss Graef's *Mystics of Our Time*, "*that the missionaries were making a great mistake in admitting, contrary to all biology, the equality of all races. . . . Creatures so different from ourselves could not be converted unless one first transformed them on the human plane.*" During his twenty-odd years in China, Fr. Teilhard never made the slightest attempt to convert any of the Chinese; Fr. North tells us that he never learned the Chinese language, and could not even write his name in Chinese.

It should be abundantly evident, therefore, from the short analysis of Fr. Faricy's book on Fr. Teilhard's *Theology of the Christian in the World* that his published writings really contained the grave errors against the faith that are mentioned in the article in *L'Osservatore Romano* of June, 1962, and that these writings are dangerous. And from the accounts of his early life by Fr. North, S.J., and by Miss Hilda Graef it is clear that he suffered from delusions of a pantheistic nature all his lifetime.

Further confirmation of this will be found in *Lettres a Leontine Zanta*, published at Paris, 1965, in one of which Fr. Teilhard wrote:

"What is going to dominate my interests as you already know, is the effort to establish within me and spread around me a new religion (let us call it, if you like, a better Christianity) in which the personal God ceases to be the great monolithic proprietor of old in order to become the soul of the world which our religious and cultural stage of development calls for."

Our conclusion, therefore, is that it is vain and foolish to attempt to construct a "Theology of the Christian in the World" from the writings of Fr. Teilhard de Chardin.

The English Translation Of The New Dutch Catechism

(Published without **Imprimatur** by Herder and Herder)

The original Dutch edition of this catechism is at present being examined by a commission of six Cardinals appointed by His Holiness Pope Paul VI to pronounce on the doctrinal orthodoxy of the catechism which has been called into question in Holland. Besides dealing with the truths which have come to us through revelation and taught by the Church, the catechism deals also directly and indirectly with scientific theories which affect the explanation of the teaching of the Church on the origin of man, polygenism and Original Sin. As the examination of the accuracy of the scientific information given in the new Dutch catechism concerning above question does not form part of the investigation to be made by the papal committee, I propose to discuss it here.

The Origin Of Man

In the Encyclical *Humani Generis*, issued by Pope Pius XII in 1950, while permission is given to people who are experts both in the natural sciences and the sciences dealing with revelation to discuss the possibility of the evolution of man's body from pre-existing living matter, it is expressly forbidden to teach the evolution of man's body from pre-existing living matter as an established fact, and it is stated in the same Encyclical that this and all other papal Encyclicals bind in conscience.

The author or authors of Part I, "The Mystery of Existence," completely ignore the directives of the *Magisterium* of the Church and state bluntly without any qualification on page 10: "The life in my body comes from the beasts."

The Proofs From Science Given By The Dutch Authors

On page 9 (bottom) and 10 (top) we read the following:

"The skulls and bones that have been found tell us something that we had not known, that the further back we delve into the past, the more primitive is the type of man we find. Before *homo sapiens*, present-day man, science distinguishes Neanderthal Man, his forehead and chin receding somewhat.

"Earlier still, over two hundred thousand years ago, there were various forms of hominids, with strongly receding facial angles, but walking upright. They had crude stone tools and they hunted.

"Three hundred thousand years earlier . . . a still more primitive type can be vaguely discerned, the Australopithecus, an ape-like being but more human than present-day apes. Nearly everything is uncertain—the dates, families, the links between the various phases. One thing stands out clearer and clearer, the marvelous fact that a species of animal living in plains and forests mounts a long, slow line of evolution to reach—us. *The life in my body comes from the beasts.*"

The above quotation acknowledges as true, at least tacitly, what is admitted by most evolutionists, including Charles Darwin and Sir Julian Huxley, that the only direct proof of evolution of species is the existence of fossils of intermediary forms usually called "missing links." It is true, however, that Fr. Teilhard de Chardin appeals to a law by which the links (which he calls peduncles) must disappear and leave no trace. Scientists do not recognize such a law, and even Fr. Teilhard himself made feverish attempts to establish two new links between man and beast in his Piltdown and Peking men, both of whom turned out to be cases of fraud.

In the quotation from the new Dutch Catechism given above, the claim is made that various forms of "hominids that walked erect" existed some two hundred thousand years ago and two specific examples are given, one a nearly perfect specimen, the Neanderthal Man, and one a doubtful case but a degree beyond a mere animal, the Australopithecus. The two specific examples are unfortunate, for the Neanderthal Man is now acknowledged to be a perfect *homo sapiens* and has been written off by prominent evolutionists; the second example, the Australopithecus, is equally unfortunate, for such authorities as Sir Julian Huxley and Sir Solly Zuckerman have written him off as being a mere animal with none of the special human characteristics. (See *Evolution as a Process* edited by Sir Julian Huxley).

With regard to the "hominids that walked erect" referred to in the above quotation, in the first place, no such thing as a hominid ever existed and no genuine fossils of such a creature have ever been found. Claims to have found fossils of "missing links" have been made repeatedly since the time of Darwin, but every single case without exception has been found to be a case of fraud or deception. The mythical hominids referred to in books by evolutionists do not walk erect; even though Neanderthal Man is still represented with his head bent forward like an ape's.

At the end of the last century, Dr. Dubois, a Dutch surgeon, went to Java to find a hominid. He found a human thigh-bone and, not far away, the skull of a gibbon, and from them composed his *Pithecanthropus erectus* (ape-man that walked erect). But admitted before his death that the skull used (from which he had removed the brain-case) was that of a gibbon. Later on Dr. Konigswald, another Dutchman, went to Java and constructed other hominids from the fossil skulls of gibbons but had no human thigh-bones and did not make them walk erect. The "hominid that walked erect" is a Dutch invention and should not have appeared in the English translation intended for the United States of America.

The Early History Of Man In The New Dutch Catechism

There is no reference to the Deluge, as an historical fact and no account of the early history of man is given; instead, we read the following on page 40:

"In the years before and after the exile, words were uttered which threw divine light not merely on the meaning of Israel's history but also on that of all mankind. The story of our origins which we now find in the beginning of the Bible (Gen. I-XI) about Adam and Eve, Cain, Noah and Babel were then given form. We shall explain elsewhere how these chapters do not ultimately intend to relate actual historical facts."

The Pontifical Biblical Commission in the responses has emphatically declared that these chapters contain history, and this has been confirmed in the Encyclicals *Providentissimus Deus* of Pope Leo XIII and *Divine afflante Spiritu* of Pope Pius XII. The excavations that have been carried out all over the Middle East since the beginning of the century by expeditions from the universities of various countries have confirmed the biblical account of the Deluge and the early history of man.

The New Dutch Catechism's Account Of Abraham And The Jewish Race

Abraham is represented as a "half-barbarian nomad" and the Jews after their sojourn in the fat of the land of Egypt for four hundred years are referred to as "a group of harried nomads who escaped from their oppressors through a dried-up waterway, a branch of the Red Sea."

Abraham came from Ur of the Chaldees and lived about the time of Hammurabi, the Babylonian conqueror and author of a code of laws. The standard of civilization of the southern kingdom of Sumeria, to which Ur of the Chaldees, the home of Abraham, belonged, was far higher than that of Babylonia and its laws more humane; Abraham could not therefore be justly called a "half-barbarian nomad." The description of the Jews at the time of the Exodus from Egypt, "as a group of harried nomads who escaped from their oppressors through a dried-up waterway" simply means that the authors of the new Dutch Catechism, having reduced the first eleven chapters of the Bible to a collection of myths, want to deprive the biblical account of Abraham and the Jewish peoples up to the time of King David of practically all historical value, admitting only that Abraham and the Jewish Patriarchs were real persons.

Original Sin In The New Dutch Catechism

The treatment of the question of Original Sin in the New Dutch Catechism is contradictory and confusing, as the following quotations show.

"Sacred Scripture speaks of "original sin." It appears most clearly in Chapters I-XI of Genesis and above all in Chapter V of the Epistle to the Romans. The first eleven chapters tell of the origins of mankind—Adam, Cain, Noah and Babel. We know that they are not descriptions of disconnected historical facts. . . . Chapters I-IX describe the basic elements of all human encounter with God. It is only with Chapter XII, where Abraham appears, that we begin to make out historical figures in the past. . . ."

The nearest thing to a definition of what constitutes Original Sin given by the Dutch authors is the following:

"Original Sin is the sin of mankind as a whole (including myself) in so far as it affects every man. In every personal sin the original sin of man is basically present and active and contributory."

It is evident from the above quotations that the Dutch authors of their New Catechism want to get rid of the testimony of the whole first eleven chapters of the Bible, and that their definition of Original Sin is not in agreement with the official teaching of the Catholic Church. The excuse, which was given in the early part of the catechism, for rejecting the historicity of the first eleven chapters of the Bible and for giving a new definition for Original Sin is the alleged existence of a race of creatures called "hominids that walked erect" in process of evolution towards the status of man. The proof for the existence of these hominids turned out to be a human thigh-bone and the fossil skull of a gibbon.

As already stated, Catholic evolutionists used to claim that there was no conflict between the theory of evolution and the doctrines of the Catholic Church. In recent years the tune has been changed; it is now claimed that there is conflict between the theory of human evolution and the traditional teaching of the Church and that it is the teaching of the Church that must be changed to bring it into agreement with the theory of human evolution as at present defined. The authors of the New Dutch Catechism leave no doubt about the fact that they want the traditional teaching of the Church on Original Sin changed, and the chief reason which give for their attitude is the alleged existence of "hominids that walked erect."

Evolution And Original Sin

by

Fr. Karl Rahner, S.J.

As stated above, Fr. Rahner was co-author with Fr. Overhage, S.J., of *Hominization* and contributed an introduction to *Teilhard and the Creation of the Soul* by Fr. Robert North, S.J., and, by doing so, gave moral support to the ideas expressed in both books. In *The Evolving World and Theol-*

ogy (Concilium Vol. 26) he contributes a chapter in his own name entitled "Evolution and Original Sin" in which, abandoning his usual reserve, he makes an excursion into the realm of science with unhappy results.

On page 64 of this book he announces his thesis as follows:

> "Thesis: In the present state of *theology* and *science* (italic type is ours) it cannot be proved that polygenism conflicts with orthodox teaching on original sin. It would be better therefore if the magisterium refrained from censuring polygenism."

Fr. Rahner's Proof Of His Thesis

His proof from theology is that Pope Pius XII "accepted" the evolution of Adam (from pre-existing living matter) and that this involved the acceptance of the evolution of Eve in the same manner as Adam, and rendered the decision of the Biblical Commission in 1909 about the formation of Eve from Adam untenable.

The following are his words:

> "The first question a theologian should seriously ask himself is: Can the Church logically . . . leave us free to accept anthropological evolution on the one hand—as she does (DS3896)—and on the other, condemn polygenism? This is the situation:

"(a) If evolutionary hominization is acceptable, we have to accept that 'Eve' came about in the same way as 'Adam'. Any other view can only be a worthless compromise. . . . The decision of the Biblical Commission in 1909 about the 'formation of the first man' is no longer tenable in its exclusive literal sense if one accepts in general with Pope Pius XII the evolutionary origin of man (which basically conflicts with this decree). We cannot think of 'Adam' in terms of evolution and deny this for 'Eve'. . . ."

"One cannot accept evolution for 'Adam' and then reject it for 'Eve'. Polygenism can therefore no longer be rejected in the case of one couple."

Reply To Fr. Rahner's Argument From Theology

It is not true, but in fact it constitutes a calumny on the memory of Pope Pius XII, to say that he accepted the evolution of Adam. Fr. Rahner is evidently referring to the Encyclical *Humani generis* of Pius XII. Before this Encyclical was issued in 1950 Catholics without any qualifications had been discussing the possibility of evolution of man from a lower animal, and indeed were claiming that it was an established fact. In the Encyclical *Humani generis*, Pius XII restricted permission to discuss the possibility of human evolution to the very limited number of people who were at the same time experts both in the field of natural sciences and the field of sacred sciences, and forbade all Catholics, including the experts, to teach as an established fact that the body of man was evolved from pre-existing living matter.

Pope Pius XII did not, therefore, accept the evolutionary origin of Adam or tolerate the opinion expressed by Fr. Rahner, that "Adam" may represent a group, for in *Humani generis* he states expressly:

"The faithful cannot embrace that opinion which maintains either that after Adam there existed on this earth true men who did not take their origin through natural generation from him as from the first parent of all, or *that Adam represents a certain number of first parents.*"

Both parts of Fr. Rahner's argument, therefore, collapse completely. His attempt to get rid of a decision of the Biblical Commission expressed so clearly on a question of fundamental importance comes under the censure of Pope St. Pius X in his *Motu Proprio* of 1907 in which we read:

> "After mature examination and the most diligent consultations, certain decisions have been happily given by the Pontifical Biblical Commission, and these of a kind very useful for the promotion . . . of biblical studies. But we observe that some persons unduly prone to opinions and methods tainted by pernicious novelties . . . have not received and do not receive these decisions with a proper obedience.

> "Wherefore, we find it necessary to declare and prescribe, as we now declare and expressly

prescribe, that all are bound in conscience to submit to the decisions of the Biblical Commission which have been given in the past and shall be given in the future in the same way as to the decrees which appertain to doctrine, issued by the Sacred Congregations and approved by the Sovereign Pontiff; nor can they escape the stigma both of disobedience and temerity, nor be free from grave guilt as often as they impugn these decisions either in word or writing and this over and above the scandal which they give and the sins of which they may be the cause before God by making their statements on these matters which are very frequently both rash and false."

Fr. Rahner's Argument From Science

"(b) (1) "How can one explain . . . that the mutual independent origin of two human beings (Adam and Eve in the supposition that they were evolved) from the animal world must be limited to these two only . . . and then how can one understand that one 'Adam' and one 'Eve', both being evolved independently of each other, without appealing to miraculous interventions by God for which there is no justification. In other words, is it seriously probable that, within the wider population unit of the immediately preceding prehominids . . . only these two break through to become human beings?"

(2) "It is doubtful, to say the least, whether a bodily historical *unity* of the first two human beings can be understood in terms of monogenism. It is a general principle of biology that true, concrete genetic unity is not found in the individual but in the population. . . .

"Only within such a situation can evolution come about since selection can exercise its pressure only within such a population and not in isolated individuals. . . ."

Reply To Fr. Rahner's Argument From Science

Father Rahner's argument is in two parts; the first assumes the existence fo a population of hominids or pre-hominids; the second part assumes the validity of the theory of Neo-Darwinism; or some similar theory, but both of these assumptions are false. (1) Scientists as such do not speak of a "population of hominids" at all; in the past some scientists thought that the fossils of a very limited number of hominids or "missing links" had been discovered, but, as has been lately shown, every case has been later found to have been a case of either fraud or error.

(2) No such "principle of biology" as the one to which Fr. Rahner appeals exists. Fr. Rahner confounds a principle of biology with an unproven assumption of the theory of Neo-Darwinism. It has been already shown that all attempts to prove

that new species can be formed from mutations in the genes guided by Natural Selection have failed.

Fr. Rahner has given no indication in any of his writings that he has carried out sufficient research in Palaeontology to justify him in expressing an opinion about whether such beings as hominids ever existed, or in biology, which would justify him in assuming that a whole group or species of animals has simultaneously evolved, first into hominids and then into men.

As has been shown in the early part of this book, scientists from Europe and America who have carried out excavations in the Middle East, where the cradle of the human race is located, since the end of the last century up to the present, have arrived at solutions of the problems of the origin and early history of man which are in perfect accord with the Mosaic account in Genesis if interpreted strictly in accordance with the directives of the Biblical Commission—which Fr. Rahner wishes to be set aside. Fr. Rahner gives no indication that he ever studied the accounts of these excavations which were written by the experts who superintended them. Can he then justly claim to be an expert in the natural sciences in the sense demanded by the Encyclical *Humani generis* which would qualify him to discuss the problems of human evolution and polygenesis?

Use Of Doubtful Arguments From Science Ruled Out By "Humani Generis"

In *Humani generis* Pope Pius XII says:

"It remains for us now to speak about those questions which although they pertain to the positive sciences, are nevertheless more or less connected with the truths of the Christian faith. In fact, not a few insistently demand that the Catholic religion take these sciences into account as much as possible. This certainly would be praiseworthy in the case of clearly proved facts; but caution must be used when there is rather question of the hypotheses, having some sort of scientific foundation, in which the doctrine contained in Sacred Scripture or in Tradition is involved. If such conjectural opinions are directly or indirectly opposed to the doctrine revealed by God then the demand that they be recognized can in no way be admitted."

In the chapter on "Evolution and Original Sin" which we are discussing. Fr. Rahner gives, in the name of science, not "clearly proved facts" as the Encyclical demands (he does not even give hypotheses with a real scientific foundation) but extravagant statements about a population of mythical hominids that have no more real existence than the goblins of the fairy tales, and an appeal to a biological principle unknown to science.

Fr. Rahner's thesis, which is, that in the present state of theology and science it cannot be proved that polygenism conflicts with orthodox teaching on Original Sin, contradicts the statement in Humani generis which says:

> "Now it is in no way apparent how such an opinion (polygenism) can be reconciled with that which the sources of revealed truth and the documents of the Teaching Authority of the Church with regard to Original Sin which proceeds from a sin actually committed by an individual Adam and which through generation is passed on to all and is in everyone his own."

Fr. Sagues, S.J., in Vol. II of *Sacrae Theologicae Summa*, rejects the opinion of those who say that the words *Cum nequaquam appareat* (Now it is no way apparent) do not rule out the possibility of further doctrinal development on the subject of Original Sin which would make the discussion of the subject (which is forbidden in the Encyclical) permissible. He points out, (1) that, while discussion of human evolution is permitted, discussion of polygenism is forbidden, and (2) that the Fathers of the Church and the great theologians are unanimous in their teaching about Original Sin and that their teaching excludes the possibility of change or modification in the doctrine.

This Vol. II of *Sacrae Theologicae Summa* in which Fr. Sagues, S.J., repects both the theory of human evolution, even in mitigated form, and the theory of polygenism, as being incompatible with the teaching of the Church, was presented to the late Pope Pius XII who sent a letter through Msgr. Montini (now Pope Paul VI) in which he said the interpretation of all papal documents, which was given in this Vol. II was scrupulously accurate.

Finally, Fr. Rahner's thesis is in conflict with the directives given by His Holiness Pope Paul VI to the theologians and scientists taking part in the symposium on Original Sin, which was published in L'Osservatore Romano July 15, 1966, and his advice to the magisterium to refrain from censuring polygenism is presumptuous and wanting in respect to the Holy Father.

The following is the concluding paragraph of the address of His Holiness to the theologians and scientists who were present at the symposium:

> "It is therefore evident that the explanations of Original Sin given by some modern authors will seem to you irreconcilable with true Catholic doctrine. Starting from the undemonstrated premise of polygenism, they deny, more or less clearly, that that sin from which so many cesspools of evil have come to mankind was first of all the disobedience of Adam, 'first man,' figure of that future Man committed at the beginning of history. Consequently these explanations do not even agree with the teaching of Scripture, of sacred tradition and the Church's magisterium, according to which the sin of the first man is transmitted to all his descendants not through imitation but through propagation, 'in each one

as his own' ('inest unicuique proprium') and is 'the death of the soul,' that is, privation and not simple lack of holiness and of justice even in newborn babies."

Fr. Francoeur and those who share his views are the victims of the intense propaganda inside the Catholic Church for the theory of evolution during the past half century.

Fr. Francoeur and the Catholic writers with views similar to his are the victims of half a century of intense propaganda inside the Catholic Church for the theory of evolution, and for an interpretation of the Mosaic account of creation and of the early history of man which ignores the directives for the interpretation of *Genesis* given in the responses of the Biblical Commission and in Papal Encyclicals. These writers are almost completely ignorant of the scientific information about the history of earliest man obtained from the labors of the organized expeditions which carried out excavations in the Middle East, the cradle of the human race, for nearly a century, for the reason already given, that the books containing accounts of the excavations are either out of print or difficult to obtain. Those who, like myself, have lived through those fifty years of propaganda inside the Church have had the advantage of being able to consult the books of the great scholars of the beginning of the century, now long out of print. The books quoted by Fr. Francoeur and the authors who share in his views make no reference to the scientific information referred to above, but give instead unproven theories and hypotheses.

Pope Pius XII, of blessed memory, in His Encyclical *Humani generis*, issued a warning against the use of such unproven scientific hypotheses when the teaching of the Church is involved, in the following statement:

"Caution must be used when there is rather questions of hypotheses, having some sort of scientific foundation, in which the doctrine contained in Sacred Scripture or Tradition is involved. If such conjectural opinions are directly or indirectly opposed to the doctrine revealed by God, then the demand that they be recognized can in no way be admitted."

Conclusion

The geologists, palaeontologists, and archaeologists who have been working since the end of the last century, each in his own department, have made available sufficient exact information to enable research workers to trace the history of man back to the Great Flood at the end of the Ice Age, and from the Great Flood back to earliest man. In particular, they have found the date of the Great Flood which is about 7,000 B.C. They have shown that earliest man was a highly enlightened man; that from primitive beginnings he rapidly invented tools, manufactured household utensils, developed the arts of painting, and agriculture, built towns and cities, and kept domestic animals, which, it may be presumed, were provided by Almighty God for our First Parents. They have shown that the nomadic tribes, like the Neanderthal, that lived in the caves of Europe and Africa, do not represent earliest man, but were men who wandered away from the centres of civilization and lived by hunting.

The various international expeditions that carried out the excavations have given us exact knowledge of the standard of civilization at the time of the Flood; they have provided us with information which shows that at the time of the Flood the bulk of the human race was confined within a relatively small area, usually called the Fertile Crescent, and that man had not crossed the Himalaya Mountains into India or China; that, after the Flood, it was in Mesopotamia that man began again; that, before the separation into various parts of the world, he had developed a system of hieroglyphic writing, which the Egyptians brought to Egypt, the Chinese to China, and the Indians to America.

Evolutionists, mostly through ignorance, tell us nothing about all this. Instead, they give us a long list of mythical creatures, half-man, half-ape, which they represent as creatures that really existed, but which have, one and all, without exception, been proved to be either cases of fraud or deception. I have already dealt with them individually.

The general conclusion is, therefore, that there is no scientific foundation for the theory that man was evolved from a lower animal or for the theory of polygenism. The books written to defend them, such as the books of Fr. Teilhard de Chardin and Fr. Francoeur, show that their authors were almost totally ignorant of the scientific discoveries made during the last century about the origin and early history of man.

Statement Of His Holiness
Pope Paul VI On The Doctrine
Of Original Sin

Extract from the address of His Holiness to the theologians and scientists taking part in a symposium on Original Sin (from the text of His address published in L'Osservatore Romano July 15, 1966).

Convinced, therefore, that the theories of Original Sin both regarding the existence and universality, its character as true sin even in the descendants of Adam and its sad consequences for soul and body, is a truth revealed by God in various passages of the Old and the New Testament, but especially in the texts you well know of Genesis 3, 1-20, and of the letter to the Romans 5, 12-19, always take care, in scrutinizing and specifying the meaning of biblical tests, to observe the indispensable norms which stem from the *analogia fidei* (analogy of faith), from the declarations and definitions of the above-mentioned councils and from the documents issued by the Apostolic See. Thus you will be certain of respecting *"id quod Ecclesia catholica ubique diffusa semper intellexit"* ("what the Catholic Church, wherever it has spread, has always understood"), that is to say the sense of the universal Church, teaching and learning, which the Fathers of the Second Council of Carthage, which concerned itself with Original Sin against the Pelagians, considered *"regulam fidei"* ("a rule of Faith").

It is, therefore, evident that the explanations of Original Sin given by some authors will seem to you irreconcilable with true Catholic doctrine. Starting from the undemonstrated premise of polygenism, they deny, more or less clearly, that the sin from which so many cesspools of evil have come to mankind was first of all the disobedience of Adam, "first man," figure of that future Man committed at the beginning of history. Consequently these explanations do not even agree with the teaching of Scripture, of sacred tradition and the Church's magisterium, according to which the sin of the first man is transmitted to all his descendants not *through imitation but through propagation*, "in each as his own" ("*inest unicuique proprium*") and is "the death of the soul" that is, *privation* and not simple *lack* of holiness and justice even in newborn babies.

Appendix

The items of this appendix were not included in the Italian translation of the original edition which was presented to His Holiness Pope Paul VI. They are as follows:

(1) Text of the Vatican Council II decree on Revelation and the Interpretation of Sacred Scripture, with brief commentary taken from *Science of Today and The Problems of Genesis.*

(2) The following extracts from *The Origin and Early History of Man*, which was published in 1965 with the Imprimatur *of Most Reverend John Kyne*, Bishop of Meath, Ireland.

    (a) False theories of our time about the interpretation of the Bible.

    (b) The Wellhausen theory.

    (c) The account of the origin of man, the flood, and the early history of man to be derived from the literatures of Sumeria and Babylonia.

Vatican Council

The following are the decrees of Vatican Council II which concern the Rule of Faith and the questions of the Inspiration and Inerrancy of the Bible. In these decrees the traditional teaching of the Catholic Church is reaffirmed.

Chapter 2—(Constitution On Divine Revelation)

"Sacred tradition and sacred scripture form one sacred deposit of the word of God, committed to the Church. Holding fast to this deposit the entire holy people united with their shepherds remain always steadfast in the teaching of the apostles, in the common life, in the breaking of the bread and in prayers, (see Acts 2, 42, Greek text), so that holding to, practising and professing the heritage of the faith, it becomes on the part of the bishops and faithful a single common effort."

TEACHING AUTHORITY OF THE CHURCH

"But the task of authentically interpreting the word of God, whether written or handed on, has been entrusted exclusively to the living teaching office of the Church, whose authority is exercised in the name of Jesus Christ. This teaching office is not above the word of God, but serves it, teaching only what has been handed on, listening to it devoutly, guarding it scrupulously and explaining it faithfully in accord with a divine commission and with the help of the Holy Spirit; it draws from this one deposit of faith everything which it presents for belief as divinely revealed.

It is clear, therefore, that sacred tradition, sacred scripture and the teaching authority of the Church, in accord with God's most wise design, are so linked and joined together that one cannot stand without the other, and that all together and each in its own way under the action of the one Holy Spirit contribute effectively to the salvation of souls."

Chapter 3—(Constitution On Divine Revelation)
Sacred Scripture: Its Divine Inspiration And Interpretation

THE MEANING OF DIVINE INSPIRATION

"Those divinely revealed realities which are contained and presented in sacred scripture have been committed to writing under the inspiration of the Holy Spirit. For holy Mother Church, relying on the belief of the apostles (see Jn. 20:31; 2 Tim. 3:16; 2 Pet. 1:19-20; 3:15-16), holds that the books of both the Old and New Testaments in their entirety, with all their parts, are sacred and canonical because, written under the inspiration of the Holy Spirit, they have God as their author and have been handed on as such to the Church herself. In composing the sacred books, God chose men and while employed by Him they made use of their powers and abilities, so that with Him acting in them and through them, they, as true authors, consigned to writing everything and only those things which He wanted.

Therefore, since everything asserted by the inspired authors or sacred writers must be held to be asserted by the Holy Spirit, it follows that the books of scripture must be acknowledged as teaching solidly, faithfully and without error that truth which God wanted put into the sacred writings for the sake of our salvation. Therefore "all scripture is divinely inspired and has its use for teaching the truth and refuting error, for reformation of manners and discipline in right living, so that the man who belongs to God may be efficient and equipped for good work of every kind. (2 Tim, 3:16-17, Greek text)."

THE INTERPRETATION OF SACRED SCRIPTURE

"However, since God speaks in sacred scripture through men in human fashion, the interpreter of sacred scripture, in order to see clearly what God wanted to communicate to us, should carefully investigate what meaning the sacred writers really intended, and what God wanted to manifest by means of their words.

To search out the intentions of the sacred writers, attention should be given, among other things, to 'literary forms.' For truth is set forth and expressed differently in texts which are variously historical, prophetic, poetic, or of other forms of discourse. The interpreter must investigate what meaning the sacred writer intended to express and actually expressed in particular circumstances by using contemporary literary forms in accordance with the situation of his own time and culture. For the correct understanding of what the sacred author wanted to assert, due attention must be paid to the customary and characteristic styles of feeling, speaking and narrating which prevailed at the time of the sacred writer, and to the patterns men normally employed at that period in their everyday dealings with one another.

But, since holy scripture must be read and interpreted in the same spirit in which it was written, no less serious attention must be given to the content and unity of the whole of scripture if the meaning of the sacred texts is to be correctly worked out. The living tradition of the whole Church must be taken into account along with the harmony which exists between elements of the faith. It is the task of exegetes to work according to these rules toward a better understanding and explanation of the meaning of sacred scripture, so that through preparatory study the judgment of the Church may mature. For all of what has been said about the way of interpreting scripture is subject finally to the judgment of the Church, which carries out the divine commission and ministry of guarding and interpreting the word of God.

In sacred scripture, therefore, while the truth and holiness of God always remains intact, the marvelous 'condescension' of eternal wisdom is clearly shown, 'that we may learn the gentle kindness of

God, which words cannot express, and how far he has gone in adapting his language with thoughtful concern for our weak human nature.' For the words of God, expressed in human language, have been made like human discourse, just as the word of the eternal Father, when he took to himself the flesh of human weakness was in every way made like men.

The Interpretation Of Sacred Scripture

IN THE DECREE OF VATICAN COUNCIL II WE READ

The interpreter of Sacred Scripture, in order to see clearly what God wanted to communicate to us, should carefully investigate what meaning the sacred writers really intended and what God wanted to manifest by means of their words.

To search out the intentions of the Sacred writers, attention *among other things* should be given to literary forms.

The decree does not specify what the "other things" are but in Divino Afflante Spiritu (of Pope Pius XII) we read the following:

[35] What is the literal sense of a passage is not always as obvious in the speeches and writings of the ancient authors, of the East, as it is in the works of our own time. For what they wished to be expressed is not to be determined by the rules of grammar and philology alone, nor solely by the context; the interpreter must, as it were go back,

wholly in spirit to those remote centuries of the East and with the aid of history, archaeology, ethnology, and other sciences, accurately determine what modes of writing, so to speak, the authors of the ancient period would be likely to use, and in fact did use.

[40] Let those who cultivate biblical studies turn their attention with all due diligence towards this point and let them neglect none of these discoveries whether in the domain of archaeology or in ancient history or literature, which serve, to make better known the mentality of the ancient writers, as well as their manner and art of reasoning, narrating and writing.

The knowledge that the information about the physical universe and early history contained in the Bible has been verified in our own time increases our veneration for the Bible and makes it easier for men to accept the spiritual truths and spiritual lessons conveyed along with it. If, as Modernists would have us believe, it could be proved that the very first chapters of the Bible, pronounced by the Church to be inspired word of God, contained only Babylonian myths used by Moses to convey spiritual lessons, respect for the Bible would soon decline. Fortunately, modern science has come to the aid of the Magisterium of the Church and has brought forward conclusive evidence in confirmation of its decisions on the interpretation of the Bible.

False Theories Of Our Times About The Bible And The Origin And Early History Of Man

The principal of these theories are: (1) That the Mosaic account of creation gives us no information about the order or the manner in which the world and what it contains were created, except that God was the Creator of all things: (2) that evidence furnished by modern Science about the origin of man makes it almost certain that Adam was evolved from a lower animal, and Eve also: (3) that the Deluge was only a local flood, and the antiquity of the human race is at least half-a-million years; and (4) that the doctrine of the inspiration of the Bible needs to be redefined and made more elastic so as to make room for the above theories.

The Truth About These Theories

Now with regard to these theories: (1) The discoveries in the domain of astronomy made during the past twenty years make it possible to explain the Mosaic account of creation as it stands, without changing the order, if we translate the Hebrew word 'yom' as a period, instead of a day of 24 hours. (2) The evidence that has come to light during the same twenty years is more than sufficient to show that the case for the evolution of man from a lower animal has collapsed; (3) the great authorities on geology, such as Sir Henry Howorth, published conclusive evidence at the beginning of the century which shows that the greater part of the Northern Hemisphere was covered with ice to a thickness of a mile to two miles and sank beneath the ocean, about 9,000 years ago, and thus caused the Deluge; and the excavations carried out during the present century, especially those carried out during the past ten years, confirm the account of the geologists; (4) therefore, the most recent scientific information confirms the account of the creation of the world and of the origin and early history of man given in the Bible and makes it unnecessary to modify the definition of inspiration based on the Decrees of the Councils of Trent and Vatican.

The Wellhausen Theory

According to this theory which takes its name from Wellhausen, (1844-1918) who was an atheist, Moses was not the author of the Pentateuch (the first five books of the Bible). According to him there were four different authors or sets of authors who wrote at different times, hundreds of years after the time of Moses, and their four accounts were combined to make these first five books, about 400 B.C. Two of these accounts or sources get their titles from the two different names for Almighty God used by the Jews, and are called the Yahvist and the Elohist sources; the third is called the Deuteronomist, from the Book of Deuteronomy; and the fourth, the Priestly Code, from the priests who were supposed to have composed it. These four sources are designated by the letters J.E.D.P. According to Wellhausen the J. source was composed between 850 and 700 B.C.; the E source, about 722 B.C., the D. source, about 540 B.C. and the P. source about 538 B.C. When combined in 400 B.C. to make one continuous account, the authorship of this combined account was ascribed to Moses by a pious fraud.

In the responses of the Biblical Commission dealing with the Mosaic Authorship already quoted, there is no mention of the Wellhausen theory, but it is virtually condemned under two headings. (1) The response states clearly that Moses is the author of these five books, with the exception of some small additions such as glosses and explanations: and (2) while the Commission makes no statement on the question whether documents were used in the composition of the Pentateauch, it allows the theory to be put forward that documents were used, provided that these documents were in existence at the time of Moses.

Some Catholic writers have adopted a modified form of the Wellhausen theory, the modifications differing according to the different writers, and it has become a subject of controversy among Catholic writers since the time of Wellhausen.

Up to a few years ago there was only one way to settle the controversy, which was to accept loyally the decision of the Biblical Commission: that Moses was the author of substantially the whole Pentateuch, and that if documents were used, they were documents that were in existence during the lifetime of Moses.

During the last ten or fifteen years discoveries have been made in various branches of science which help to refute the Wellhausen theory and which support the decisions of the Biblical Commission.

The Account Of The Origin And Early History Of Man To Be Derived From The Literatures Of Sumeria And Babylonia

The excavations of the cities of the Middle East show that there was no system of writing in existence before the great Flood at the end of the Ice Age, and hence that there is no written account of earliest man that dates back before the Flood.

The first system of writing, which was hieroglyphic, was invented within the first thousand years after the Flood, probably about 6,000 B.C. This system continued to be used in Mesopotamia until the alphabetical system was invented more than four thousand years later; it was brought to Egypt, China and America in a developed form at the time of the dispersal, which proves that the ancestors of the Egyptians, the Chinese and the American Indians had been in Mesopotamia together after the flood.

The first place to be occupied after the Flood was the fertile valley between the Tigris and Euphrates in which the first post-Flood cities were built and the first kingdoms were established. The first two of these kingdoms were: Sumer (generally known as Sumeria), in the south, and Akkad in the north. The kingdom of Sumer or Sumeria lasted for 5,000 years until it was conquered by the people of the North who changed the name to Babylonia and made Babylon, which was the first city built after the Flood, the capital.

How The Ancient Writing Was Preserved

As no paper was available, clay tablets were used instead. The inscriptions were written on these, and they were then baked and put in order. Tens of thousands of these baked tablets have been found during the excavations and have been given to the museums of Europe and America where the inscriptions on a great number of them have been deciphered and published.

The most important of these tablets for our present purpose are those which give a list of the kings of Sumeria both before and after the Flood down to the time of the first dynasty of Babylon, and those which contain the earliest account of the Flood that has come down to us. Both of these sets of tablets date back to only about 2,000 B.C. which is 5,000 years after the Flood. The list of kings contain merely the names of the kings and an indication of the length of their reigns.

The Sumerian Account Of The Flood

Baked clay tablets containing an account of the Flood were first discovered during the excavations of the ancient city of Niniveh that were carried out between 1849 and 1854. These belonged to the library of King Assurbanipal (668-726 B.C.) and were deciphered and published by George Smith in 1876. It was thought at the time these tablets were published that they dated about a thousand or at most two thousand years afer the Flood. It is now known that more than 5,000 years elapsed between the Flood and the time of King Assurbanipal. Other tablets containing an account of the Flood that date back to about 1,900 B.C. have since been found; these contain substantially the same account and were also written 5,000 years after the Flood. It is true that they are at least five hundred years earlier than the time of Moses, but Moses, who was brought up at the court of the Egyptian Pharao, could not have seen them or consulted them.

The account of the Flood to be derived from these tablets is just what might be expected from genuine descendents of Noe, (as the unknown scribes that wrote the inscriptions on them certainly were) who lived 5,000 years after the event, and who depended on oral tradition. This account says: that Noe, whom they call "Uta Napisthim" was ordered by the gods to build a great ship and to put into it "all his gold and silver" (which were not used at all before the Flood) and "the seeds of life." The ship was in the form of a perfect cube, 120x120x120 cubits with nine decks, and carried all Uta Napisthim's family and relations, his boatman and all his craftsmen. The flood was caused by rain alone which lasted only six days. Uta Napisthim sent out a dove, a swallow and a raven to reconnoitre, and on the seventh day he offered

sacrifice to the gods. The unknown scribe attrib-
utes the account to a historic personage named
Gilgamesh, who was the fifth king of the First
Dynasty of Arach. Gilgamesh is represented as
having received the account from Uta Napisthim
who had become a god after the Flood.

At the time the account was recorded, the Su-
merians had become polytheists and worshipped a
number of gods, but according to Sir Leonard
Woolley and Professor Langdon, both of whom
superintended excavations in Mesopotamia, there
is evidence from the strata immediately above the
Flood deposit, to show that the first descendents
of Noe worshipped one God only. When they in-
creased and built new cities, these new cities each
claimed to have their own gods, and thus poly-
theism had its beginning.

A Comparison Between The Accounts Of (1) Moses, (2) The Scientists And (3) The Babylonian And Sumerian Scribes

MOSAIC ACCOUNT	SCIENTIST'S ACCOUNT	SUMERIAN ACCOUNT
Almighty God warned N o e a n d ordered him to build the Ark. Noe's Ark was oblong in form: 300x 50x30 cubits.	No information. No information about the Ark.	The gods warned Uta Napis-thim and told him to build a ship. Uta Na-pisthim's ship was cubic in f o r m : 120x 120x120 cubits.

Cause Of The Flood

An incursion of the sea, accompanied by 40 days' rain.	Submergence of the Northern hemisphere probably accompanied by rain.	Rain for six days only.

Duration Of The Flood

One year.	Several months, probably a year.	Seven days only.

MOSAIC ACCOUNT	SCIENTIST'S ACCOUNT	SUMERIAN ACCOUNT

Extent Of Flood

MOSAIC ACCOUNT	SCIENTIST'S ACCOUNT	SUMERIAN ACCOUNT
''The waters were 15 cubits higher than the mountains which they covered'' and must therefore have been of immense extent.	The Flood extended to Europe, Africa, the plains of India and China, the Arctic Ocean and North America.	No information about the extent of the flood.

Other Circumstances

MOSAIC ACCOUNT	SCIENTIST'S ACCOUNT	SUMERIAN ACCOUNT
Noe sent a raven first and then a dove at intervals of seven days. He offered sacrifice to God.	No information about birds or sacrifice. Remains of a ship have been found on Mount Ararat.	Uta Napisthim sent out a dove, a swallow and a raven at unspecified intervals. He offered sacrifice to the gods.
The Ark landed on Mount Ararat. (Note on page 14).		

In an expedition to Mount Ararat in 1955, in search of Noe's Ark, the explorer Fernand Navarra discovered a quantity of hand-hewn beams of white oak embedded in ice at an altitude of 14,000 feet, which he estimated to be about 50 tons in weight. Some of the beams were from 150 to 200 feet long and were curved as if for a ship.

These beams must have belonged to Noe's Ark for the following reason. The only time in the history of the human race that it was possible for a ship to land on Mount Ararat at an altitude of 14,000 feet was when Noe's Ark, according to the Bible, landed there. Modern scientists have fixed the date of the historic flood which covered Mount Ararat once and never again at about 7,000 B.C.

The waters of the Flood would have melted the ice and snow on Mount Arart before the Ark landed. When the waters of the flood had receded, the snow that fell in the course of time covered the mountain and the Ark, and have never since melted again as in the case of the frozen mammoths (referred to on page 14) which have been preserved in ice since the flood, the ice and snow on Mount Ararat have preserved the timbers of the Ark to the present day.

An American expedition with modern drilling equipment is at present being arranged.

This discovery made in our times confirms the accuracy of the Mosaic account in a most marvellous manner, and demonstrates that the whole human race, except those on the Ark, really perished in the waters of the flood that was more than 14,000 feet deep.

From the above it appears that the most important parts of the Mosaic account, which are, the cause, duration and extent of the Flood, have been confirmed by the scientists, and that the same parts of the Sumerian account have been proved to be inaccurate. The details of the warning, the dimensions of the Ark, the sending out of the birds and the sacrifice to the gods in the Sumerian account are such as might be expected from a descendent of Noe who wrote his account 5,000 years after the event.

The Mosaic account, which was written five hundred years later than the Sumerian account, gives accurate information in simple language about the causes, extent and duration of the Deluge, which was not known even by scientists until the beginning of the present century. Since Moses could not have got this information from natural sources, he must have got it by revelation from God.

The statement by the French writer, André Parrot that the Mosaic account was derived from the Sumerian or Babylon accounts, which has been copied by Dr. Bruce Vawter and some other Catholic writers is, therefore, without foundation.

Conclusion

The fact that the Biblical account of the origin and early history of man is confirmed by the results of the investigations of geologists, archaeologists and palaeontologists carried out during the last century, and that the account of the evolutionists has no real scientific support, but is largely based on fraud and deception, justifies the strong action taken by St. Pius X, Pius XII and other

Popes in defense of the account of the origin and early history of man given in the first eleven chapters of the Bible. The Holy See has never recognized the claim of evolutionists based on the now discredited Wellhausen theory, that there are two accounts of the creation of man and two accounts of the Deluge, and that Chapter I is an addition to the Bible made at a later date. The Magisterium of the Church has made it a defined doctrine that the Bible and all its parts contains truth without error of any kind, and that those parts dealing with the origin of the world and the origin of man are covered by inspiration equally with the parts that treat of faith and morals.

Mosaic Account Of Creation Confirmed By Present-Day Science

Modern science has not only confirmed the Biblical account of the origin of man, but also of the origin of our earth. According to the Biblical account strictly interpreted, the earth and the sun were created separately. The science of the last ten years has proved that the sun is composed of 99% hydrogen, and hence that it would be impossible to form the earth from it, as was taught by the Laplace theory, and wrongly applied to interpret the Bible. What was formerly a theory put forward by Newton three hundred years ago has been confirmed by the observations made by the great telescopes of Mount Wilson and Jodrell Bank, that the sun had its beginning in the form of fiery nebulae spread out over hundreds of millions of miles. In his address to the Pontifical Academy of Sciences delivered on Nov. 22, 1951, Pius XII speaks of: "The work of creative omnipotence, whose power, set in motion by the mighty *Fiat* pronounced billions of years ago, spread out over the universe, calling into existence with a gesture of generous love matter bursting with energy. In fact, it would seem that present-day science, with one step back across millions of centuries, has succeeded in bearing witness to that primordial *Fiat Lux* uttered at the moment when, along with matter, there burst forth from nothing a sea of light and radiation, while the particles of chemical elements split and formed into millions of galaxies."

In thus appealing to modern astronomical discoveries to confirm the accuracy of the Mosaic account of creation given in the very first verses of Genesis, His Holiness is putting into practice the principles He laid down in His Encyclicals *Humani Generis*, and *Divino Afflante Spiritu* in which He said that Catholic scholars, while avoiding the use of unproved theories to interpret the Bible, should avail themselves of genuine scientific discoveries that help to bring to light its real meaning. Evolutionists do just the contrary of this; they apply their theory of evolution and the Wellhausen theory to interpret the first chapters of Genesis, but protest loudly against what Pius XII advocates, namely the application of scientific conclusions to confirm the Biblical account: they call this "Concordism" and warn their readers against it as if it were a dangerous form of heresay.

We are, therefore, justified in concluding that the discoveries in the various branches of modern science, especially those made in the last twenty years confirm the biblical account of the origin and early history of man which says that man was formed from inanimate matter directly by God and that the present human race is descended from a single pair of ancestors. There is therefore no scientific foundation for the contrary theory of polygenism, and there is no need to modify the teaching of the Church on Original Sin.

List Of Books Consulted

(This list is taken from the Italian edition which was Presented to Pope Paul VI.)

Rome and the Study of Scriptures: Collezione degli Atti Pontifici sullo studio delle Scritture, con le decisioni della Commissione Biblica.

The Theory of Evolution Judged by Reason and Faith, Card. Ruffini, New York, 1959.

Introductio in Libros Sacros Veteris Testamenti, F. B. Mariani, Roma, 1958.

Introduction Generalis in Sacram Scripturam, H. Hopfel, O.S.B., ed. Ludovicus Leloir, Napoli e Roma, 1958.

La Sainte Bible, Commento di P. Louis Pirot e Can. Clamer, Paragi, 1953.

A Catholic Commentary on Holy Scripture, London, 1953.

God, Man and the Universe, Ed. Jaques de Bivort, London, 1954.

Origines: (Genese, Ch. I-III), P. Charles Hauret, Paris, 1953.

Apologetics and Catholic Doctrine, and The Origin of Life, by Archbishop Sheehan, D.D. Dublin, 1950.

Les Origines de L'Homme, Nicolas Corte, Paris, 1957.

The Bible, Science and Faith, Rev. J. A. Zahm, U.S.A., 1895.

Theologie de L'Ancien Testament: L'Homme, Rev. P. Van Imshoot, Paris, 1955.

Sacrae Theologiae Summa, PP. Gesuiti Spagnoli, Madrid, 1952.

La Lecture Chretienne de la Bible, Dom Celestin Charlier, Paris, 1959.

The Christian Approach to the Bible, Traduzione inglese di La Lecture Chretienne de la Bible, London, 1958.

Guide to the Bible, Peres Robert et Tricot, Paris, Tournai, Roma, New York, 1955.

Introduction a la Bible: Introduction General Ancien Testament, Peres Robert e Feuilliet e Cie, 1957.

L'Evolution: Hypothesis et Problems, Remy Collin, M.D., Paris, 1958.

Problemes D'Origines, P. M. Grison, Paris, 1954.

L'Uomo Nello Spazio e Nel Tempo, P. Marcozzi, S.J., Milano, 1953.

Le Origini Dell'uomo, P. Marcozzi, Milano, 1954.

Hacia el Origin del Hombre, P. Anderez, S.J., ed. P. Ezpondaburu, S.J., Santander, Espagna, 1956.

Modern Discovery and the Bible, A. Rendle Short, London, 1953.

The Church and Science, Sir Bertram Windle, London, 1918.

Darwinism and Catholic Thought, Can. Dorlodot, trad. Dr. Messenger London, 1922.

Evolution and Theology, Dr. Messenger, London, 1931.

Theology and Evolution, Dr. Messenger, London, 1949.

The Bible and the Early History of Man, Fr. Humphrey Johnson, London, 1947.

The Bible as History, Werner Keller, trad. inglese, London, 1947.

A Path Through Genesis and God's Story of Creation, Fr. Bruce Vawter, London and Dublin, 1957.

The Church and Modern Science, Rev. Patrick J. McLoughlin, Dublin, 1959.

Quelques Souvenirs Sur le Movement des Idees Transformistes, Compte Begouen, Paris, 1947.

L'Origines des Etres Vivants: L'Illusion Transformiste, Louis Vialleton, Paris, 1930 (15a ed).

Oeuvres de Pierre Teilhard de Chardin, S.J.

L'Apparition de L'Homme, Paris, 1957.

The Catholic Encyclopedia, U.S.A., 1908.

Les Hommes Fossiles, Marcellin Boule, Paris, 1923.

Les Hommes Fossiles, Boule et Vallois, Paris, 1952.

Evolution: Geschichte Irer Probleme und Erkennisse, Walter Zimmerman, Munich, 1953.

The Nature and the Universe, Fred Hoyle, London, 1953.

The Story of Science, Henry W. Dietz, Cleveland, U.S.A.

Les Premiers Hommes, Bergounioux et Glory, 1952.

El Hombre Fosil, Obermaier, 1925.

On the Earliest Representatives of Modern Mankind Discovered On the Soil of East Asia, Weidenreich, Peking, Nat. Hist. Bull., 1939.

The Origin of Species, Charles Darwin, con Introd. di Dr. W. R. Thompson, F.R.S., Everyman's Library, 1959.

The Descent of Man, Charles Darwin, London, 1874.

Man's Place in Nature, T. V. Huxley, London, 1863.

Modern Biology and the Theory of Evolution, E. Wasmann, S.J., trad. ingl. A. U. Buchanan, London, 1910.

Evolution for John, H. Ward, London, 1926.

Man, A Special Creation, Douglas Dewar, 1926.

Is Evolution Proved? discuss, tra. D. Dewar and
H. S. Shelton, London, 1947.

A Challenge to Evolutionists, Douglas Dewar.

Species Revalued, Desmond Murray, O.P., London,
1955.

Natural Species, A. C. Cotter, S.J., 1947.

Evolutionary Philosophy, F. Gerard, S.J., 1904.

The Revolt of Reason, Arnold Lunn, 1949.

Man and the Vertebrates, A. S. Romer, 2 Vol.
Penguin ed. 1945.

Adam's Ancestors, L. S. B. Leakey, 1953.

Evolution in Action, Sir Julian Huxley, 1953.

Evolution as a Process, ed. Sir Julian Huxley, A.
C. Hardy and E. B. Ford, 1954.

Darwin Is Not for Children, Vera Barclay, 1950.

Challenge to Darwinians, Vera Barclay, 1951.

Apes, Giants and Men, F. Weidenreich, Chicago,
1945.

Biology and Man, F. G. W. Knowles, London, 1950.

A New Theory of Human Evolution, Sir Arthur
Keith, London, 1949.

A Second Book of Biology, Phillips and Cox, London, 1940.

The Piltdown Forgery, J. S. Weiner, Oxford, 1955.

The Piltdown Fantasy, Francis Vere, London, 1959.

Lessons of Piltdown, Francis Vere, London, 1959.

Biology of the Vertebrates, Walter S. Sayles, New
York, 1954.

Historical Aspects of Organic Evolution, Philip G.
Fothergill, London, 1952.

*El Hombre Prehisorico y Los Origines de la Hu-
manidad*, Madrid, 1944.

Gregorianum, Roma, 1948-1958.

A New Type of Fossil Man, Dr. Broom and Robinson, Nature, 1949.

Early Man in China, P. Teilhard de Chardin, Peking, 1941.

On An Adolescent Skull of Sinanthropus Pekinesis, Palaeontologia Sinica, Pechino, 1931.

Problems of the Old Testament, Mons. John E. Steinmueller, D.D., L.S.S., Bruce Publishing Co., 1936.

The Two-Edged Sword: An Interpretation of the Old Testament, J. L. McKenzie, S.J., Bruce Publishing Co., 1955.

The Fossil Evidence for Human Evolution, W. E. Le Gros Clark, Chicago, 1955.

A Hundred Years of Evolution, G. S. Carter, Sidgwick and Jackson, 1958.

Thinking About Genesis, Margaret T. Monroe, London, 1953.

Das Stammesgeschichtliche Werden der Organismen und des Menschen by the German Jesuit Fathers. Published by Herder in 1959.

The Bible, Word of God in Words of Men, by Fr. Jean Levie, S.J., London, 1961.

Dating the Past, by F. E. Zeuner, London, 1952.

Ur of The Chaldees, by Sir Leonard Woolley, London, 1950.

Digging Up the Past, by Sir Leonard Woolley, London, 1950.

Excavations at Ur, by Sir Leonard Woolley, London, 1954.

The Track of Man, by Henry Field, London, 1953.

Foundations in the Dust, by Seton Lloyd, London, 1955.

What Mean These Stone? by Millar Burrows, 1956.

Archaeology of Palestine, by W. F. Albright, New York, 1956.

Twenty-five Years of Mesopotamian Discovery, by M. E. L. Mallowan, London, 1956.

The Aztecs of Mexico, by G. C. Vaillant, London, 1956.

Lost Cities, by Leonard Cottrell, London, 1956.

Egypt and Western Asia in the Light of Recent Discoveries, London, 1907.

Excavations in Turkestan, by Raphael Pumpelly, 2 Vols., 1904.

The Testimony of the Spade, by Geoffrey, Bibby, London, 1957.

From Stone Age to Christianity, by W. F. Albright, New York, 1957.

Antiquity of Man, by Sir Charles Lyell, 1863.

Ancient Hunters, by Professor Sollas, 1924.

Men of the Old Stone Age, by Henry Fairfield Osborn, New York, 1916.

The Origin and Antiquity of Man, by G. F. Wright, London, 1912.

The Glacial Nightmare and the Flood, two vols. by Sir Henry Howorth, London, 1893.

Ice or Water, three vols. by Sir Henry Howorth, London, 1905.

The National Geographic Magazine, from 1948 to 1958.

La Pensee Catholique, Paris, 1948-1958.

Lecture on the Flood entitled *Scientific Discoveries of the Deluge,* by Col. L. M. Davies, D.Sc., F.G.S., London, 1930.

Iran, by K. Ghirshman, London, 1954.

The Story of Jericho, by John and J. B. E. Garstang, London, 1940 and 1948.

Le Deluge Biblique Devant la Foi, by Abbe Motais, Paris.

Who Perished in the Deluge? by Fr. Sutcliffe, S.J., London, C.T.S., December, 1956.

Antiquity, December, 1956. Article on the Excavations at Jericho by Dr. Kenyon.

New Light on the Most Ancient East, by V. G. Childe, London, 1952.

The Flood and Noah's Ark, by Andre Parrot. English Translation, London, 1955.

A Century of Excavation in the Land of the Pharaos, London, (no date).

Other Lumen Christi Books

THE ORIGIN AND EARLY HISTORY OF MAN
by Rev. Patrick O'Connell   **$1.00**

A review of the Church's teaching and of the scientific evidence concerning man's origin and antiquity. A discussion of evidence for the Deluge is included.

THE HOLY EUCHARIST
by Cornelius Hagerty, C.S.C., Ph.D.   **$1.50**

A thorough explanation of the Eucharist which reviews the Church's traditional teachings and appraises some recent theories and approaches.

THE AUTHENTICITY OF THE SACRED SCRIPTURES
by Cornelius Hagerty, C.S.S., Ph.D.   **$6.00**

A survey of the Bible which reviews its history and its content, refutes its adversaries, and offers proof for its authenticity and veracity.

PRIESTLY CELIBACY: RECURRENT BATTLE AND LASTING VALUES
by Albert J. Hebert, S.M.   **$6.00**

A positive approach to the celibate priesthood, dealing with the reason for its being, its importance to the Church, its effect on vocations and its significance for the laity. The author discusses the theological and psychological aspects of celibacy.